Christian Freedom
for
WOMEN*

and Other Human Beings

Harry N. Hollis, Jr.
Vera Mace
David Mace
Sarah Frances Anders

BROADMAN PRESS
Nashville, Tennessee

To all those, both women and men, who have
seen the vision of a world where Christian womanhood can develop its full potential, and who are
pursuing that goal with courage and dedication.

Library of Congress Catalog Card Number: 74-21566

Dewey Decimal Classification: 261.8

Printed in the United States of America

Preface

"Women's lib: no! Adam's rib: yes!" This is how I heard a speaker put it recently. But surely this is a dangerous over-simplification of the human struggle that females and males face today. It is a clever continuation of the put-down of women. It ignores the injustices to females which many in women's liberation movements are trying to correct. And it perpetuates the erroneous view that the Bible teaches the utter subordination of women.

*Christian Freedom for Women * and Other Human Beings* is a Christian response to the human problems faced by females and males in our society. The title of this book is more than window dressing. It is a clue to what we are trying to do here. The focus is on Christian freedom, not just on women's libera-tion. Although we will zero in on women's freedom, the larger purpose is to talk about men and women, boys and girls—all human beings. The thrust of this book is that all human beings can find freedom through Jesus Christ, the true liberator.

Last August a group of men and women gathered at the Glorieta Conference Center in New Mexico to consider ways of speaking to the problems which women and men face in our society. This conference was sponsored by the Christian Life Commission of the Southern Baptist Convention. These pages contain the presentations of the two women and two men who led this conference.

The gathering at Glorieta demonstrated that many Christian people are committed to working within the church to bring about justice for women and true *koinonia* between women and men.

At the end of this book is a section entitled "Questions for Further Study." Groups which get together to raise consciousness about issues related to the freedom of women and men can use the questions in that section as discussion starters.

To Foy Valentine, Executive Secretary of the Christian Life Commission, the authors of this book are grateful. Dr. Valentine has worked courageously through the Christian Life Commission to apply the gospel to all matters of morality. His leadership made this conference possible. And his commitment to freedom for all humans gives hope and a rallying point to all who want to work through churches to bring about creative change.

We are also grateful to the people of Broadman Press for their decision to be a part of the struggle for human freedom by publishing this book.

The authors appreciate the helpful way in which Mrs. Pauline Barnard directed the preparation of this manuscript. She was ably assisted by Mrs. Gaye Eichler, Mrs. Annette Hayward, and Mrs. Faye Russell.

Today an increasing number of people are seeking justice for women. Christianity in its best expression seeks justice plus something else: genuine love. This book is written in the belief that the love inspired by Jesus Christ is our best hope for Christian freedom for all human beings.

Harry N. Hollis, Jr.

Contents

1
Women and the Family in the Bible

Vera and David Mace

In this inquiry into the life of women, past and present, we shall be trying to understand the Christian point of view. We two will confine most of what we have to say to one area of woman's life—her role as wife and mother. The other two writers will range widely over other areas of the life of woman.

Of course, in reality, this division of women's roles is not to be encouraged. Indeed, one of the sins of society is that it has tried to confine woman to one of these areas and to exclude her from many of the others. However, from the point of view of trying to present our material clearly, this division of functions seemed to us, in our planning, to be a convenient one. Among the various writers there will inevitably be some overlapping; but we will try as far as possible to stay within the boundaries we have agreed upon.

As Quakers, who have greatly enjoyed working with Southern Baptists over a period of many years, we have learned that in the discussion of any subject, it is always best to begin with what the Bible says. This makes good sense to us, and it creates no problems. We have studied carefully what the Bible teaches about sex, marriage, and the family. *Hebrew Marriage* [by David Mace], published in 1953 and now out of print, was accepted at the time by most authorities, both Jewish and Christian, as a valid interpretation of what the Bible has to say about women; and some of the ground was covered again in the later book, *The Christian Response to the Sexual Revolution* [also by David Mace], published in 1970.

Let us make two introductory comments by way of explaining what we will be trying to do. First, there can be as many interpretations of the Bible as there are readers of it, and we are inevitably not going to agree about everything. However, our hope is that this book will help us all move toward some degree of agreement on the major questions concerning the role of women in Christian society. What we contribute to the discussion will arise from personal conviction; but being Quakers, we always speak with an open mind, ready to learn new truth and ready to change our views if deeper and clearer understanding comes to us.

The second comment is that, in the space of one chapter, we cannot possibly deal with all that the Bible says about women. This, however, doesn't trouble us. We often learn best from the Bible by trying to see it as a whole, and not in its several parts. So we shall try in this discussion to focus on the issues that sum up for us the Bible doctrine of womanhood.

When we study the Bible on almost any subject, the usual procedure is to work first through the Old Testament, and then the New Testament. We prefer for this discussion to begin with Jesus himself. Fortunately, his teaching on this subject seems to be perfectly clear. It has often been observed that the attitude of Jesus to women is in striking contrast to that of most of the world's greatest religious teachers and leaders. Again and again, he spoke warmly and tenderly of the woman's role in the family. He entered into close relationships with women like Martha and Mary and in a quite unorthodox fashion. He took time out to sit and chat with the woman at the well. He even befriended a prostitute and was criticized for it. In his dying moments on the cross, he was concerned to make provisions for his mother to be cared for after his death. The overall picture in his relationships with women leaves us in no doubt at all that he accorded them honor and respect to a high degree—and not only as wives and mothers but also as *persons.* We stress this fact because it has often been conveniently ignored by church leaders. This must be the point at which we begin and the point to which we continually return.

This point need not be elaborated further. All objective investigators have agreed about it. Anyone who sets out to build a case for the subordination of women knows he isn't going to get much support from the Gospels and soon turns to the Old Testament and to Paul. So, with that picture of the example of Jesus clearly in our minds, let us now go back to the Old Testament, as we must do in studying all questions of Christian social policy.

The Hebrew View of Women

Ryder Smith, an eminent British Bible scholar of earlier days, published a book in 1923 entitled *The Bible Doctrine of Womanhood.* The book is a thoughtful one, and still worth studying; and if we disagree with some of his interpretations, we mean no disrespect to him. The position he took was that throughout Old Testament times we can trace a gradual evolution from the view that saw women as chattels, "items of property," to a more mature attitude that regarded them as fully developed persons. Our objection is that we don't believe the Hebrews ever *did* treat their wives as property. The view that they did so has often been expressed, but we believe it is based on a whole series of misunderstandings.

Let us just pick out a few of these misunderstandings. The first is in the Commandment which says, "Thou shalt not covet thy neighbor's wife." "There you are," someone says, "you see, the wife is treated like a piece of furniture, just like the ox and the ass and other items of property." This is not true. A moment's thought will make it clear that the Commandment is not referring to a Hebrew who looks out at his neighbor's wife as she works in the field and says: "My, that's a fine, strong, muscular woman! I wish I could have her to work *my* cabbage patch!" Nor is he saying: "That Sarah next door sure is smart with her needle! I wish I had her to sew on *my* buttons!" Of course not. What he *is* saying is: "She's a real sexy woman. Wouldn't I like to go to bed with her!" What he is coveting is her *sexuality.* And it was the Hebrew view that a husband had exclusive rights to his wife sexually. But that doesn't mean that he treated her person as a piece of property.

Of course, there *were* women in the Old Testament who were badly treated by their husbands. And that is still true today. But today, it is argued, the wife has *rights.* She can go to the court and get justice. So she could in Hebrew times. The Old Testament law, if you study it closely, protects the wife in all sorts of ways. The unfortunate women who had no protection were the slave women—those who had been captured in war or sold into bondage. We're not defending the Hebrews because some of them kept concubines. But we are asking you not to assume from this that they treated their wives badly and that the wives had no redress. That just wasn't true.

So let's lay to rest the illusion that Old Testament wives were treated as chattels. It simply is not supported by any solid evidence. We shall have more to say about this later.

The Subordination of Women

What *is* true is that the Hebrew woman was considered, as a person, to be *subordinate* to the man. There are some interesting reasons for this. Let us discuss three of them.

In the Bible, God was always viewed as masculine. So, if God is a man, we may naturally conclude that any man is more like God than any woman is.

But are we justified in thinking of God as a sexual being? The old Greeks thought of their gods that way, and there were some strange goings-on up there on Mount Olympus! This was also true of many of the peoples surrounding Israel; but the Hebrews always reacted with horror to such ideas.

What need would God possibly have of sex? He has no body, no need to marry, no need to beget children. When the Bible talks of Jesus as the only begotten Son of the Father, we are only using human language to describe something that is literally "out of this world." So, when the Bible talks of man as being made in God's image, the word used is not the one used for masculine man but for *humanity*, both man and woman.

Of course, there is the biblical story about the woman being made from Adam's rib. This could easily suggest that woman would be less important than man, because she was formed out of only one part of his body. But this could be a very dangerous argument, because every man since Adam has in fact been formed out of a part of a woman's body! So we had better face the fact that what God made was both a man and a woman, to be equally partakers in his nature. He made them sexual beings in order that they might multiply and people the earth. He himself had no need of sex because he was the Creator.

The Hebrew view of reproduction. It hasn't occurred to most people that the Hebrews, although they had a very positive and healthy attitude toward sex, had almost no scientific understanding of the sexual function. Having no microscopes, they simply drew conclusions from what they could observe. So, of course, they knew nothing about the sperm and the ovum. They took the view that it was the man's seminal fluid that produced the baby, but that in order to do so it had to be deposited in the woman's body, which acted as an incubator, nourishing it with her blood. She took over the baby from the man at a very early stage, and then returned it in a much more advanced state of development. What this meant was that, to the Hebrews, the woman contributed nothing of her essential self to her future child. She therefore played an inferior role in the all-important drama of reproduction.

It is our belief that this underlying concept explains, better than any other, the Hebrew view of the woman's subordination. If she played a secondary, auxiliary role in reproduction, then it followed that she must be a secondary, auxiliary type of person. The whole patriarchal system, which pervades Old Testament society, is based on this belief.

But now we have microscopes, and we know more about the way God made us than the Hebrews did. We know that both the man and the woman contribute an equal number of chromosomes and genes to the making of their child. (Actually, because of the Y chromosome, the man contributes slightly fewer genes.) So the whole structure of superiority and inferiority collapses in the light of our fuller knowledge today; just as the Hebrew idea that the earth was flat, and that the sky covered it like an overturned bowl, collapsed when our fuller knowledge gave us an understanding of outer space. This new knowledge, both of what was too small for the Hebrews to see and what was too big for them to see, has made the work of God's creation more marvelous than it could ever be in their eyes. But we need to correct some of the false conclusions we have drawn from the imperfect understanding of the past. If we now accept the reality of outer space, we ought also to accept the equal roles of men and women in the founding of a family.

Eve and the serpent. Tradition has often suggested that woman is weak because Eve was beguiled by a serpent in the Garden of Eden. But wasn't Adam equally beguiled by Eve? He didn't *have* to eat the forbidden fruit just because she did. God didn't declare Eve to be guilty and Adam to be innocent. He blamed them both equally and punished them both equally.

Can we be so sure that if the serpent had gone first to Adam, instead of to Eve, he would have responded any differently? Eve was attracted to the forbidden fruit for three reasons— because it seemed to offer a good meal; because it was attractive to look at—it made her mouth water; and because it promised to make her wise—like a god, the serpent said. Now, who will dare to suggest that a man is more likely than a woman to turn his back on a good meal? Or to reject something that is desirable? Who will suggest that man, as distinct from woman, is lacking in the ambition to get ahead and to improve himself? Let's face the simple fact. Both Adam and Eve did wrong, and both were punished.

So what's all this about the man ruling over the woman? It involves two concepts, one biological, and the other psychological. The first has to do with woman's vulnerability. The man is usually physically stronger than the woman; and when the woman is pregnant, she needs protection because she is vulnerable. She also, as a mother of young children, needs protection. So in primitive times the man's protective role was important, and the woman had to accept the role of being dependent upon him.

The second concept has to do with basic sex roles. Despite all that has been said to the contrary, throughout nature the male is the initiator in the sex act, while the female's function is to respond. It is true that this difference in sex roles has been exploited and exaggerated; but it contains a nucleus of truth which we cannot discard, because it is based on differences in physiology and in biology.

Because of the differences in their reproductive roles, therefore, there are two different kinds of relationships between men and women. As male and female, their relationships are reciprocal and complementary—and this is the way they want it and like it. As persons, however, they are equal. Both of these relationships are valid, and we don't have to choose the one or the other. But we don't have to mix them up either. And that's just what we have been doing. Let us explain.

In the ancient world, the reciprocal relationship was the most prominent one, because in a continual struggle for survival the woman really needed a protector. Unfortunately, men made use of this fact to gain power over women and applied it not only to the masculine/feminine interaction, where it belonged, but also extended it to the relationship of persons in society, where it didn't apply. By doing this they suppressed the equal relationship of persons, and wrongfully denied women their personhood. *Now, today, we are in danger of swinging to the opposite extreme. We now stress the equality of persons so much that we may be in danger of suppressing the reciprocal masculine/feminine interaction.*

These are, we think, the important aspects of the Hebrew view of woman. They explain why we don't often find women playing leadership roles in the Old Testament—largely because there just weren't any opportunities to be anything other than wives and mothers. Really, apart from being married, a Hebrew woman had just about two alternative choices—to be a prophetess or to be a prostitute; and we find Hebrew women in both roles. If you think all Hebrew women were treated as chattels, you might find it profitable to read again the story of Deborah in Judges 4–5. She was a prophetess. As she sat under that palm tree on Mount Ephraim, we are told that the children of Israel came up to her for judgment. By contrast, it took our Christian society a long time to appoint the first woman judge! And the remarkable thing was that Deborah was a married woman. Somehow, she managed to hold a position of high prestige in the community and to be a homemaker as well!

But Deborah was a very unusual woman. Let's take a look at the average Hebrew wife and mother.

Boys and girls married young in Old Testament times— probably quite soon after puberty. Why not? There were no schools or colleges to attend. The training of the girl was almost exclusively in homemaking, and she got it from her mother. So when she was old enough to have children, she was ready for marriage. The marriage was arranged by her parents and the parents of her future husband, because marriage in those days was a matter between families rather than of personal choice. As in some Eastern countries even today, the young people trusted their parents' judgment rather than their own. But good parents would obviously try to make an arrangement that would bring happiness to their children. And don't imagine that romantic love was despised in Bible times. After all, the Old Testament includes a whole book of love songs, and there is another such song in Psalm 45.

When a girl's marriage had been arranged, she and her future husband were betrothed. This was an agreement between the two families that the marriage would take place at some future time, and it was sealed by the payment of the *mohar* or "bride-gift." This was usually a sum of money paid to the bride's father; but it could be paid in property, or even, as in the case of Jacob, in labor.

Some people have called this the "bride-price," and argued that it meant that the girl was bought from her father, and that this supports the idea that the wife was really a chattel.

This is quite mistaken. The *mohar* served two purposes. First, it compensated the father for the loss of his daughter, because she now left her parents to devote herself to the building up of her husband's family. But on rare occasions the bride-gift could serve another purpose. If the marriage for some reason turned out to be unsatisfactory, the husband might divorce his wife and return her to her father. In that event, if it could be proved that the girl had been at fault, the father had to return the bride-gift. If, however, it turned out that the husband had treated his wife badly, her father could take his daughter back and keep the bride-gift as well. So the *mohar* provided a sort of defense against the wife being badly treated in her husband's home. The wife had another safeguard in the form of the *dowry*, which was given to her by her father on the occasion of her marriage. This might take the form of money, or precious stones, or household goods. It was normally considered the wife's exclusive property, and it provided her with something of her very own that she could cash in if she fell on evil times. But of course if she found herself in serious trouble she could always return to her own family, where her kinsmen would be bound to make provision for her needs.

All these wise arrangements show us clearly how false is the idea that Old Testament wives had no rights. They had privileges as persons that were jealously safeguarded. The wife was in a completely different position from the slave or bondwoman.

The wife's true fulfillment in Old Testament times was of course to give her husband children, especially sons to continue his family name and line. This was of vital importance, and a barren wife was in serious trouble. The Hebrews believed that conception wasn't just the result of sexual intercourse. They had a very healthy and indeed highly spiritual view of sex. They believed that God personally participated in the sexual union of husband and wife, opening the womb when he regarded the wife with favor and closing it to show his displeasure. To fail to conceive was therefore something like a curse. We can understand vividly what this meant from Rachel's heartbroken cry—"Give me children, or I die!"

Once she had borne children, the Hebrew wife was in a privileged position. It was true that she had little power outside the family; but life in those simple rural communities was centered in the home—and in the home, the wife and mother was queen. In addition she had rights and privileges. For example, her husband had to meet her sexual needs, which were regarded as equal to his own. Even a slave-woman taken by a Hebrew as a concubine must not be denied her sexual rights, as is made clear in Exodus 21:10. How much more therefore must he not deny his wife's sexual needs. You will remember that Paul the apostle, who is accused by many of being rather negative about these matters, makes it clear that married couples must not deny each other their sexual rights (1 Cor. 7:5).

The Hebrew wife could also expect *companionship* from her husband. The creation story in the book of Genesis stresses the fact that both man and woman bear the divine image, and therefore have a common nature. It also explains that God created woman because, "It is not good that the man should be alone," and because none of the animals could provide the companionship he needed.

The peasant life of the Hebrews probably encouraged this husband/wife companionship. Sharing the hard work of growing food from the rocky soil of Palestine would require close cooperation and understanding. (We usually find that the life of small farming communities fosters good marriage relationships.) There are several Old Testament passages in which men sing the praises of the good wife; however, it must be admitted that there are also a few references to unfortunate men whose wives were hard to live with!

We need add very little about the Hebrew woman as mother. Motherhood was her supreme joy, for children were regarded as the gift of God and a great blessing. The word "child" was one of the most joyful words in the Hebrew language, and there is no sign in the Old Testament of the cheap estimate of children which we find among other ancient peoples. There is, for example, no reference to induced abortion anywhere in the Old Testament, and we can be sure that the Hebrews would have regarded it with horror.

All in all, therefore, the Hebrew wife and mother had a very good life. She was cherished and respected, and she enjoyed many privileges. The distinguished biblical scholar, W. A. L. Elmslie, summed it up: "In Jewish homes, women attained an honor and dignity without parallel in antiquity."

Women in New Testament Times

We need add very little about women in New Testament times. We have already made it clear that Jesus, following the proud tradition of his people, treated women with the greatest dignity and respect. And it seems very clear that he expected the church he founded to do the same. Unfortunately, later Christians have not always followed their Master in this respect.

In closing a word must be said about the apostle Paul. There is no record that he ever married, although a traditional rumor has suggested that he was jilted by the high priest's daughter and that this accounts for his lack of enthusiasm for married life! But this is unfair to Paul, because his attitude toward women is not nearly as negative as has been suggested.

Of course Paul reflected the traditional Jewish view that women should play a subservient role, especially in public. But his views on sex and marriage were greatly influenced by a very important factor. Paul believed that the end of the world was near at hand. For this reason, family life and having children seemed to be of little importance. What mattered was that every Christian believer should be ready for the final judgment. It is unfair to Paul to interpret what he said about the conditions of human life without recognizing this.

So, with the end of the world approaching, being married or not being married was no longer important. Each believer must do as he thought best, and Paul had more urgent things to attend to than giving detailed instructions about how to manage Christian families. All the same, he made his position unmistakably clear in a resounding declaration which no one can challenge. In Galatians 3:28 he said in the plainest language possible that all distinctions of race, class, and sex are violations of the Christian gospel. Among Christians, he said, "There is neither male nor female, for you are all one in Christ Jesus." This towering affirmation leaves us in no possible doubt, because it sums up for us the whole teaching of the Bible. The Old Testament prepared the way. Jesus exemplified it in his whole life. The church has failed sadly to honor it; but it remains at the very heart of the Christian message.

It is hard to escape the conclusion that the doctrine of the subordination of woman is false doctrine. It springs not from the heart of the Christian message, but from the ideas, customs, and attitudes of ancient peoples who dimly perceived the truth, and who could not free themselves from their traditional shackles. The story of the creation, properly understood, presents man and woman as equals—equal in being formed in the divine image, equal in having sinned and fallen from a state of grace. The life and teaching of Jesus presents man and woman as equal recipients of his love and respect. The clearest and most unequivocal utterance of Paul, the first and greatest of all Christian missionaries, presents man and woman as equal in the new world order which Christ had established. And until the church, clearly and without hesitation, gives to men and women the full equality which the Bible proclaims, its message to the world will not be the full gospel which it was commissioned to preach.

So let us conclude by repeating Paul's final, clear, and definitive statement, the meaning of which cannot be in doubt: "Before faith came, we were confined under the law, we were kept under restraint. But now that faith has come, we are no longer under a custodian. For as many of you as were baptized in Christ have put on Christ. There is neither male nor female, for you are all one (without distinction) in Christ Jesus."

2
Changing Responsibilities of Women in the Church

Sarah Frances Anders

For over a decade now, a considerable proportion of the thirty-thousand book titles appearing annually have been dedicated to the causes of liberation—for blacks, for the environment, for the Chicanos and Indians, for nations, and for the "second sex." The greatest book on liberation, however, has been around for hundreds of decades and is the most inspired of all, able to speak to the needs of any oppressed group. Unfortunately, the Bible—written, compiled, and interpreted almost exclusively by men—has most often been misused by the church it spawned to support and authorize subjection of various classes of persons. In no instance has this been more true than in the church's treatment of women.

While nowhere near complete, the revolution of roles is underway for women in most spheres of the contemporary world; and women in almost every faith are challenging their ecclesiastical authorities to take another look at Eve and to move over to make room for women in new church roles. They suspect that far too much has been made theologically of the fact that while man was utterly consumed with the high-level sorting and labeling of all the living species for God the Creator, woman was puttering around the Garden daydreaming, sentimentalizing, or, perhaps worse, scheming to get her way and lead man astray. Yet this sort of man-woman arrangement has been the continuing and universal model whether in the home, labor force, arts, sciences, or religion.

Make no mistake, women's liberation *is* abroad in the land and the church must not drag its feet! The spirit of the movement within the church began probably in 1969 as an informal caucus of women, realizing that men have been long determining the theology of their position and experience in the church, stated:

Nowhere is the situation of women better illustrated than in our male-dominated and male-oriented churches. The church, both in its theology and in its institutional forms, is a reflection of culture. It has shown no propensity to transcend culture as regards the status of women although it knows that it ought. Indeed the church has too often maintained anachronistic attitudes and practices long after other societal institutions have begun to shift.[1]

This is not the time to call for a theology of women, for that would be no more appropriate to the New Testament ethic than a theology for any other minority group. Nor is this the place to review the Scriptures and develop an apologetics for the use of male pronouns for the God-head persons and female gender for the church, grace, and the "birther" of Jesus. We need not even recount the small number of women in the Old Testament who appeared to throw off the limitations imposed on them by a strongly patriarchal Hebrew society. For the prophetesses like Deborah (Judg. 4:4,5), Miriam (Ex. 15), Huldah (2 Kings 22:14-20), and Noadiah (Neh. 6:14) did not participate in or make decisions in the rituals of the services as priestesses would.

There are numerous women recorded, without the appearance of having been "singled" out as exceptionals, who figures prominently in the organization and leadership of the early church. These go beyond the women who lived in narrow Judea and shared three years of intimate friendship with Jesus; they include women in all parts of Europe who worked and traveled with Paul, who perhaps has been wrongly accused of misogyny. Consider Apphia, possibly the wife and co-worker of Philemon (Philem. 2) who had the church in their home. Most familiar is Priscilla, good business partner in tentmaking and missions with her husband Aquila and Paul in several churches (Acts 18). Then there were Dorcas, called a disciple in Joppa (Acts

9:36-43); Lydia, a successful merchant, who made her home in Philippi headquarters for Paul and Luke (Acts 16); and Nympha, a single woman who opened her house for the church (Col. 4:15). When Paul singled out twenty-eight good friends and church leaders for greetings in his letter to the Romans, eight of those were women. At least sixteen prominent church women were mentioned in Acts and the Epistles. Apparently, there was no need for him to admonish them in manner of speech or dress, for they were clearly distinguished from the women of the street and led out in the church with dignity and power.

Dale Moody has pointed out three ministries that were among those distinctive to the woman in the New Testament church, all three yet to be included in the program of a contemporary church. First were the special services performed by the unmarried women (1 Cor. 7:25-38), who were free to leave this ministry at any time if they wanted to marry. Then there were the widows who did good works in the name of the church, which supported them and defined their roles (Acts 6:1; 9:39,41; 1 Tim. 5:9-16). Last were the deaconesses, who shared the same duties as the deacons since no distinction is made. It is not unlikely that along with Phoebe (Rom. 16:1), Priscilla (Acts 18:2,18,26), Euodia and Syntyche (Phil. 4:2-4) were among those who served in this capacity.[2]

The women continued in places of prominence and service in the church for a few centuries. In the second century, Justin Martyr used deaconesses to carry sacraments to the sick.[3] About A.D. 300, the Didascalia Apostolorum of Syria stated that deaconesses were to visit in the homes of unbelievers, visit the sick, prepare women for baptism, and care for the poor; and then it further proclaimed, "And the deaconess shall be honored by you in the place of the Holy Spirit."[4]

The church in later centuries, and indeed up to the Reformation, moved toward beliefs and practices reminiscent of the ritual laws of the early Jews concerning the impurity of women during menstrual periods and post-partum, traditions Jesus obviously rejected when he dealt with the woman who had a twelve-year history of "issue of blood." Some of the ensuing taboos against women participating at the altar or even in the sanctuary because of "uncleanness" linger in some of the Orthodox churches of the East and to some extent in the more formal churches of the West.[5]

These centuries were the "Dark Ages" for women more than for civilization. What the German barbarians defined as woman's total existence—the four spheres of *kinder* (children), *kleiden* (clothing), *kuche* (kitchen), and *kirche* (church)—became the "Big Four K's" that would circumscribe her life for more than fifteen hundred years. Her only "flight to freedom" eventually came in the religous sphere, although not in the church *per se*. The monastic life became a means for what Erich Fromm would call "freedom from *and* freedom to," in that the convent provided woman not only a religious calling denied to her in the church proper, but also a place where she could study, teach, heal, and pursue the arts. She could serve selflessly but also with dignity, serenity, and exhilarating fulfillment. Every century produced women destined to be immortalized by history, but these exceptional women who rose above the drab subservience of the masses of women were often associated with the conventual movement.[6]

In the New World where there were neither convents nor religious orders for women yet, the Quakers, Baptists, and Universalists were among the more tolerant of women assuming leadership roles. Although the first woman known to have preached in America, Ann Hutchinson (1591-1643), was a Baptist, and the first woman to be ordained in 1853, Antoinette Brown (1825-1921), was Congregationalist, the majority of renowned women ministers were among the Quakers and Universalists.

Among the best-known Quaker preachers were Lucretia Mott (1793-1880), the ardent suffragist, and her contemporary, Sybil Jones, who was reputedly "easier to listen to" than her husband-minister, Eli.[7] Among the Universalists who pastored, led out in their denomination, and wrote brilliantly were Mary Livermore, Olympia Brown, and Phebe A. Hanaford, all nineteenth-century contemporaries. As early as 1770, Bedford Baptist Church, the oldest congregation in the Strawberry Baptist Association of Virginia, had deaconesses; and women in the denomination were often credited with prophetic gifts.[8] Not to be overlooked is the fact that only in the social climate of America in the 1700's and 1800's could women have founded indigenous sects. Ann Lee, reared in the Quaker tradition, attracted to her communal group a simple, dedicated people who would pioneer not only in celibacy among Protestants but also in numerous industries and the marketing of pharmaceutical herbs. Thought to be beautiful and inspired by many, she led with confidence her group that would be derisively called the Shaking Quakers or simply the "Shakers." It was almost predestined to extinction by its failure to procreate new members.[9] Some forty years later, Mary Baker Eddy, a Congregationalist who preached her first sermon in a Baptist church, would discover Christian Science and found a sect that would flourish into a large and international denomination.[10]

For the most part, women on the "second world" were helpmeets to their minister husbands or doers of charitable deeds in the parish. Many, nettled by the restraints at leadership in the local church, set their eyes upon the "uttermost parts of the earth." And where, indeed, would the modern missionary movement have been without the mite-boxes, the mission societies, and the lives laid down by such as the three wives of Adoniram Judson in Burma and by Lottie Moon in China? The amazing ability of women for raising missionary funds and for finding leadership opportunities in auxiliary church organizations was their major "flight to freedom" in the nineteenth-century Protestant churches.

Women and the Contemporary Church

The urgency of the woman's movement in the church of the twentieth century is fettered no longer by the abolitionism and suffragism of the nineteenth century nor even the civil rights movements for other minorities in the 1960's. This urgency is seen in the studies on the status of women inaugurated by most of the major denominational and ecumenical bodies within recent years. When the World Council of Churches organized in 1948, one of its initial tasks was beginning to study "The Status of Women in Church and Society." The United Nations adopted the Declaration of Women's Rights, a Preamble with eleven articles, in November, 1967, and recently set 1975 as International Year of the Woman. With women under such current scrutiny, is the research spotlight significantly changing their status in the church?

Most denominational records do not differentiate membership by sex, but the proportion of women members is probably above 50 percent as evidenced by the 57.5 percent among Presbyterians.[11] Yet many women bemoan their low representation on the full spectrum of committees and boards of the local church. This is particularly obvious among the ministry, the professional church staff, and the governing boards such as deacons and elders.

The Ministry. One of the most controversial questions in the church today is that of the ordination of women to the ministry. Some of the less liturgical churches are positioned with the Roman Catholic and the Episcopal churches in restricting women to nonclerical roles. Then there are the Congregationalists, Universalists, Methodists, and Quakers who ordained women and permitted them to hold pastorates in the nineteenth century. One newsmagazine estimated that there are seven thousand women ministers.[12] It seems likely that most of these serve in sects indigenous to America, such as Christian Science, a denomination that does not "ordain its practitioners," Aimee Semple McPherson's Church of the Four Square Gospel, and most Pentecostal groups.

The more traditional denominations that began to ordain women ministers after 1950 did so slowly. Presbyterians, North and South, had begun to ordain women before they merged into the United Presbyterian Church, but their combined number of ordained women is probably less than 1 percent of their total clergy. Both the Lutheran Church in America and the American Lutheran Church had affirmed the ordination of women by 1970, so their total number of women seminarians has only recently exceeded one hundred. Women were given full clerical rights by the United Methodist Church in 1956, but in the 1970's, women have remained less than 1 percent of their ministers.[13]

American Baptists have been ordaining women for eighty years, but the number of women pastors has fluctuated between twenty and thirty-five for many years. As one ABC report stated: "One cannot talk of deterioration in the status of women in the pastoral ministry because they have never had any status. The ABC seems to have operated on the premise that they have fulfilled their obligation to women if they ordained them."[14] The first woman ordained by a Southern Baptist church (1964) later became a pastor of an American Baptist church; and now a decade later, the total number of women ordained by Southern Baptist churches is thirteen. None of these pastor a church, but one New York City church that has both ABC and SBC affiliation has a woman minister.[15]

A part of this picture is the fact that most seminaries have not encouraged or openly recruited women for the pastoral or theology degrees. Most of the women students are enrolled in religious education or music programs, as indicated by 72.5 percent among Presbyterian women graduates and by almost 80 percent among recent Southern Baptist seminary alumnae. Some Presbyterian women graduates become pastors, associate or assistant pastors, and institutional chaplains. One Presbyterian Special Task Force report on women recommended exploration of new ministries for women as in abortion and contraception counseling, work with singles, and other chaplaincies.[16] For the denominations that have been admitting women to seminary education for years, the percentage of women has been steadily declining. A study of the Southern Baptist and

American Baptist seminaries, 1950-70, showed a decline from 17.1 percent and 16.7 percent respectively, to 10.6 percent and 8.2 percent. These proportions were still higher than the 5.7 percent for all theological seminaries in 1970, but they were significantly lower than the proportion of women (35.6 percent) in all U. S. graduate programs.[17]

When the American Lutherans made their dramatic change in attitude toward the ordination of women in 1970, a precedent was set when they proclaimed that women should be encouraged to study at the seminaries and that sex stereotypes must be offset. "Men and women are to live and serve together as full participants in all aspects of the gospel." [18]

Professional Church Staff. In spite of the preponderance of women seminarians in education and music programs, there is little to foster optimism about their positions on local church staffs. Indeed, the ABC report on women observed that "while women are encouraged to go into Christian Education, only about one-fourth of all local Directors of Christian Education are women." [19] This area of Christian service, which once was so attractive to Southern Baptist women, is now declining in its appeal. Emily Filipi has reported that women are leaving SBC church positions because of differential salaries, lack of secretarial help, and very poor fringe benefits.[20] The UPC report found it no better for Presbyterian staff women and indicated that their professional women were turning to social work, day-care centers, and teaching, because of disparities in local church working conditions.[21]

The Deaconship. Governance boards in most denominations have historically had "For Men Only" signs on them. Presbyterians, stronger on lay rule than many Protestant churches, reported in 1970 that 72 percent of their churches had women elders on their sessions. Presbyterian women considered these 17,832 women "token representation," since the average number per church was only about two, but the proportion grew to 73.5 percent by 1973.[22] Southern Baptists lag behind in the ordination of women deacons primarily due to tradition and prejudice more than theological support. Glenn Hinson, in a definitive statement of the issue, states that from the study of the early church one cannot build a perfect case either for or against the practice; but from the principle of equality within the New Testament churches and the presence of women deacons reported in some of them, positive approval is warranted.[23] Southern Baptist churches in at least nine states and Washington, D. C., are known to have ordained women and at least one church has had a chairwoman of the board. Still, the two to three hundred estimated to have women deacons seem a minute segment of the thirty-four thousand churches in the Convention.[24]

Women as Denominational Leaders and Employees

The representation of women in the higher echelons of the total work-force may seem small—38.6 percent of the professional and technical workers, 15.4 percent of the managerial workers; but when compared to the participation of women in top-level denominational positions, it seems impressive! The National Council of Churches has had women in leadership roles since its organization in 1950. Women have headed Presbyterian bodies and recently the United Church of Christ elected a black woman, Associate Justice Margaret A. Haywood of the District of Columbia Superior Court, as moderator.[25] When Mrs. Ruth Rohlfs became president of the ABC in 1972, she was the fifth woman to hold that position in sixty-five years.[26] Many groups have had no women in key positions on the national level. The SBC has had neither a woman president nor executive-secretary in its history. The only woman executive-secretary of an agency heads the auxiliary organization, Woman's Missionary Union. A woman has served as president of the District of Columbia Baptist Convention, which also prescribes that all Convention committees be evenly divided among clergy, laymen, and laywomen.

Executive Boards. Many denominations now have women serving on their denominational boards and committees, but the proportions are minimal again. At the executive board level, the ABC and the Disciples of Christ have been more favorable to women, since they compose 24 percent and 32 percent respectively, of the policy-making bodies.[27] The SBC now has only two (3 percent) women on its Executive Committee.[28]

Other Denominational Committees and Boards. The ABC probably has led most denominations in placing women on key boards and commissions, reporting about 20 percent by the early 1970's.[29] SBC women reached 5.5 percent representation by 1974, which meant there were only 50 among the 891 persons serving on 24 boards and committees.[30] It appears that women have indeed been relegated to second-class membership on the denominational level of policy-making.

Although many religious bodies are seeking an equitable distribution of laypersons and ordained members of their boards, this too will operate against female representation, assuming that the ordination of women remains rare and that women would constitute, at best, only one-half of the laypersons in the ideal 50-50 ratio of laity and clergy. Southern Baptists are probably not atypical in their present distribution of ordained members (56.7 percent), laymen (37.7 percent) and laywomen (5.5 percent). But SBC women comprise only 13 percent of the laypersons on the committees and boards, whereas ABC women make up about 35 percent of laypersons serving on their governing bodies. At best, it appears that ecclesiastical decision-making is male and clergy dominated! It is significant that women figure more prominently on missionary boards, as clearly indicated for the SBC in their 18 percent and 15 percent representation on the Home and Foreign Mission Boards, respectively.[31]

Women Among Denominational Employees. When women have been hired in denominational work, it has often appeared to be in response to "Do you type?" "Could you run a goodwill center?" "You'll be working only with women and children." The proportion of women in the national labor force is approaching 40 percent, but they are declining as a religious workforce, partially because they have not been actively recruited and partially because they are replaced by men when they retire or resign. Reorganization often causes their status to diminish.

Concern over the deteriorating position of women, particularly in the administrative positions of denominations, was justified by the findings of a survey of the employment status of women in 17 denominations and covering 65 different boards and agencies. Only 25 percent of the 1,558 positions in these organizations were held by women, but four-fifths of the respondents maintained women were not excluded by definition! A majority claimed that they had some women in executive positions, but that the proportion of men and women employees had not changed significantly in the last ten years, nor did they expect a change in the coming decade. Although 80 percent believed that women were equal in performance to men, less than 10 percent of the women with executive titles were making $15,000 or more. Yet almost 25 percent of the men were in that income range. On the other hand, more than 43 percent of the women were in the lower administrative and income positions in contrast to only 16 percent of the men. In the words of the report, "These data reflect adherence to the rhetoric of equality of opportunity for women and men on the one hand, and the factual conditions of considerable discrimination, on the other." [32]

Both major Baptist denominations saw a decline in their women personnel on a convention-wide basis in the 1960's. SBC women employees dropped from 28.2 percent to 24.7 percent of the total employees, and the ABC experienced a decline in women personnel from 21.2 percent to 19 percent.[33] However, by 1974, out of 1,444 SBC employees, 437 or 30 percent were women, and the trend seemed to be reversing.[34]

Women seemed particularly invisible in the management and executive levels during the 1960's. There were 45 SBC positions carrying titles that implied top-level administrative duties in 1971 and only three women (6.7 percent) were in them. Some restructuring apparently took place in the SBC, for by 1974, 131 positions were included under the title "management," and 36 women (27 percent) were included in this category.[35] Present hiring and promotion policies appear more favorable to women.

The Division of Christian Social Concern of the ABC reported that there had been no top-level woman executive in any ABC agency, 1958-1970. Moreover, in the five levels "A" through "E" below executive secretary in the administrative hierarchy, women were heavily concentrated in D and E levels (83 percent), which included departmental associates, staff assistants, and trainees. Women made up only 5 percent of the department heads. When the women's missionary organizations merged with the American Baptist Foreign Mission Society and the American Baptist Home Mission Society in 1955, women administrators were replaced by men as they retired or resigned. The push to recognize blacks in the leadership of the denomination no doubt will reduce the possibilities of women at higher levels.[36]

Summary

Jesus may have taught and practiced the equality of persons, but his church is far from being an egalitarian institution in this last quarter of the twentieth century. Feminists feel that sexism so permeates our churches that men and women alike have been brainwashed to think that male/female is an ordained dualism as polar as God/Satan. Yet the situation is not so bad as Margaret Mead implied, "Religious dedication is now called by psychiatric names and the dedicated *(women)* are suspected of neuroses." [37]

The new women's liberation should have begun in the church. Instead, while the secular movement to free women from discrimination in all institutions is far from complete, the church lags behind to a disturbing degree. What is the concise situation report?

1. Sexism is widespread in most Christian churches, if not in policy, surely in custom and practice. While a decided majority in most congregations and denominations, women are a

decided (and often silent) minority in most levels of leadership and decision-making.

2. Equality in the church will not deny male/female distinctives nor will it produce a unisexual church. It will provide equal opportunity for all persons to participate in any sphere of organized religion on the basis of gifts and abilities, rather than gender.

3. Ordination of women is still highly controversial, with both opponents and proponents claiming Scriptural bases on the issues. The fact is that there are many types of ministries in the pastorate and deaconship for which contemporary women are equally or better equipped.

4. Seminaries are a masculine subculture, with predominantly male professors, language, texts, trustees, and administration. Until this changes, women who train for most professional church positions will be marginal people, and to a great extent, unemployable.

5. Equal opportunity for employment is not present in most ecclesiastical structures. Not only is the percentage of women personnel low compared to the secular labor force, women seldom rise above clerical, editing, and associate administrative positions to the highest executive positions.

6. In denominations that have a congregational form of denominational power structure, "spiritual feminism" may have to move first in changing policies and practices in a significant number of local churches before the larger denominational bodies will be pressured to support the innate worth and rights of all persons, women included.

Notes

1. Women's Caucus, General Assembly of the National Council of Churches, 1969; quoted by Sally Bentley and Claire Randall, "The Spirit Moving: A New Approach to Theologizing," *Christianity and Crisis*, February 4, 1974, p. 3.

2. Dale Moody, "Is Man Superior to Woman?" *Baptist Message*, June 30, 1973, p. 3.

3. Elsie Thomas Culver, *Women in the World of Religion* (Garden City, N.Y.: Doubleday, 1967), p. 70.

4. R. Hugh Connolly, *Didascalia Apostolorum* (Oxford: Clarendon Press, 1929), p. 88.

5. Cf. Arlene Swidler, *Woman in a Man's Church* (New York: Paulist Press, 1972), p. 46.

6. Edith Deen writes of some 60 great women during this period in *Great Women of the Christian Faith* (New York: Harper and Bros., 1959).

7. Georgia Harkness, *Women in Church and Society* (Nashville: Abingdon Press, 1972), p. 113.

8. William L. Lumpkin, "Role of Women in 18th Century Virginia," Southern Baptist Historical Society meeting, Birmingham, Ala., address, quoted in Baptist Press release, April 27, 1973.

9. Deen, *op. cit.*, p. 159.

10. *Ibid.*, p. 218.

11. Report of the Standing Committee on Women and the Task Force on Women. Adopted by the 1972 UPC General Assembly (184th), *The Journal*, Part I, p. 30.

12. "Faith of Our Feminists," *Newsweek* 76 (Nov. 2, 1970), p. 81.

13. Cited in Situation Report, *Time* 99 (March 20, 1972), p. 63.

14. Elizabeth J. Miller, "Retreat to Tokenism, A Study of the Status of Women on the Executive Staff of the American Baptist Convention" (Division of Christian Social Concern, Valley Forge, Pa., October, 1970), p. 15.

15. Compiled from Baptist Press releases, 1964-1974.

16. 1972 UPC Report, *op. cit.*, p. 33; and correspondence from the SBC seminary registrars, Summer, 1974.

17. Norman Letsinger, *The Women's Liberation Movement: Implications for Southern Baptists*, Dissertation, Southern Baptist Theological Seminary, 1973 (Ann Arbor, Michigan: University Microfilm), pp. 176, 333.

18. W. L. Thorkelson, "ALC Affirms Women," *Christian Century* 89 (Nov. 8, 1972), pp. 1135-1137.

19. Miller, *op. cit.*, p. 15.

20. Emily Filipi, "What's Happening to the Women?" *The Quarterly Review* 30 (April-May-June, 1970), pp. 35-36.

21. 1972 UPC Report, *op. cit.*, pp. 10, 34.

22. *Ibid.*, pp. 27-30; and "Women Still Battling for Rights in the Church," *State-Times* (Baton Rouge, La., Sept. 8, 1973), p. 2-A.

23. Glenn Hinson, "On the Ordination of Women as Deacons" *The Western Recorder* 146 (April 1, 1972), pp. 3 f.

24. Cited in *The Deacon* 3 (April-May-June, 1973), pp. 13-14.

25. *State-Times, op. cit.*

26. "Ruth Rohlfs, Convention President," *Home Missions* 43; (May, 1973), p. 45.

27. *Ibid.*, p. 46; and Swidler, *op. cit.*, p. 73.

28. *SBC Daily Bulletin*, LI (June 12, 1974), pp. 7-8.

29. Letsinger, *op. cit.*, p. 320.

30. Porter Routh, letter to Executives of all SBC Agencies, May 2, 1972.

31. Letsinger, *op. cit.*, p. 155; and Routh, *op. cit.*

32. Earl D. C. Brewer, "A Study of Employment of Women in Professional or Executive Positions in the Churches at a National Level," *Information Service* XLVIII, No. 12 (May 31, 1969) National Council of Churches of Christ in the U.S.A. pp. 7-8.

33. Letsinger, *op. cit.*, p. 157.

34. Charles Woodward, Personnel Department, Sunday School Board, SBC, letter, June 24, 1974.

35. Letsinger, *op. cit.;* and Woodward, *op. cit.*

36. Miller, *op. cit.*, p. 11.

37. Quoted in Ann F. Scott, *Women in American Life* (Houghton-Mifflin, 1970), p. xii.

3
A Theology for Human Liberation

Harry N. Hollis, Jr.

Praised be God that he has not created me a Gentile; praised be God that he has not created me a woman; praised be God that he has not created me an ignorant man.—A Jewish prayer

Man is willing to accept woman as an equal, as a man in skirts, as an angel, a devil, a baby-face, a machine, an instrument, a bosom, a womb, a pair of legs, a servant, an encyclopedia, an ideal or an obscenity; the only thing he won't accept her as is a human being; a real human being of the female sex.—D. H. Lawrence

Too many people want to look at woman in the light of the fall rather than in the light of incarnation and redemption.—Dale Moody

Many theologies of the past, which were written by men and for men, are being crowded by new theologies which shape God in woman's image. Margaret N. Maxey is one of many who call on theology to perform a liberating task by developing "a Theology of Women which . . . would reconstruct or propose new models for woman's (and man's) self-understanding." [1] Maybe such theologies of women are inevitable responses to male-centered theologies of the past, but they are misguided for two reasons. First, they make the mistake of earlier theologies in allowing preoccupation with gender to dictate beliefs about God. Second, they precipitate a male backlash which leads to ever more masculine views of God.

Desperately needed today are theologies which move beyond a focus on males or females to a focus on *human beings.* Any approach which seeks to use God as a means to the political end of male or female domination must be rejected. Truth will be best served and justice will come more rapidly in the Christian community and everywhere when theology points toward the God who has made us human beings. This is true because, as Harvey Cox points out, "God's cosmic purpose is the liberation and maturation of all human beings, and indeed of all creation, to full participation in an ecstatic universe of love and joy." [2]

What we will examine here is a theology which liberates us to join God who is at work in the world. Throughout the Bible runs the theme that God is active in the universe, calling all human beings to respond to his activity. God is not a passive, dozing Buddha who has little interest or concern about daily affairs. God is interested in everything that he has made, and he has made everything.

The Bible teaches that God acts as Creator, Judge, and Redeemer. We are called to respond to his activity which makes it possible for us to be the human beings he intended us to be. As Harvey Cox has reminded us in *On Not Leaving It Up to the Snake*, Adam and Eve were guilty in the Garden of Eden of listening to the snake. Instead of demonstrating their full humanity by doing what God intended, they let the snake tell them what to do. Instead of talking to the animals, they let the animals tell them how to behave. They weaseled out on their humanity. They refused to be what God wanted them to be.

People still choose slavery instead of liberation, apathy instead of involvement, self-imposed prison instead of God-given freedom. What needs exploration is theology for human liberation. It is a liberation for all people—for males and females, for young and old, for rich and poor—for everyone. A Christian theology of human liberation must not be based on law, or common sense, or anything other than a relationship to the God who is active in our midst. The unique contribution that Christians have to make to the just cries for liberation is to share the good news that all human beings can be liberated through the God who is active in Jesus Christ.

We will explore here a theology for human liberation based

on God's action in the world as Creator, Judge, and Redeemer. And we will look at the human response which the divine activity demands.[3]

Creation

The Bible teaches that God is active in the world as Creator. His creative activity has implications for a theology of human liberation.

God's Action as Creator

One implication of God's creativity is that he has brought everything into being out of nothing. This teaching of *creatio ex nihilo*—creation out of nothing—means that God did not take evil matter and mix it with good spirit to make human beings. Rather, he made everything out of nothing, and thus everything he made is good. First Timothy 4:4 puts it this way: "For everything created by God is good, and nothing is to be rejected if it is received with thanksgiving." So, it is good to be a human. God made us, and we bear his stamp of approval: "And God saw everything he had made, and behold it was very good" (Gen. 1:31).

God's creative actions also relate to the differentiation of humanity into male and female: "So God created man in his own image, in the image of God he created him; male and female he created them" (Gen. 1:27). Indeed, the only "not good" uttered by God during creation concerned the fact that man was alone: "Then the Lord God said, 'It is not good that man should be alone; I will make a helper fit for him' " (Gen. 2:18).

Being a helper does not imply that the woman is inferior to the man. The Hebrew word for helper is *'ezer* which is used in many ways to refer to God, to man, and to animals. Theologian Phyllis Trible interprets this creation passage as follows: "God is the helper superior to man; the animals are helpers inferior to man; woman is the helper equal to man." [4] The Bible teaches, therefore, that male and female are different, but equal. God labored with dirt to create man and with a rib to create woman. Both required raw materials plus divine activity to be shaped into human beings.[5]

This biblical teaching stands firmly against the Gnosticism of *The Gospel of Thomas* which says: "Simon Peter said to them: Let Mary go out from among us, because women are not worthy of the life. Jesus said: See, I shall lead her so that I will make her male, that . . . she too may become a living spirit . . ., resembling you males. For every woman who makes herself male will enter the Kingdom of Heaven." [6]

The Bible teaches that it is good to be a human being because God planned it that way. Georgia Harkness points out that woman and man share the traits characteristic of the human spirit: "love, reasoning, educability, goals and their pursuit, responsible freedom, conscience, language and communication, artistic appreciation and skills, laughter—all these are as fully present in the female as in the male sex unless their exercise has been stifled through social pressures." [7]

Being created male and female makes possible the relational aspects of sex: "Therefore a man leaves his father and his mother and cleaves to his wife, and they become one flesh" (Gen. 2:24). Fellowship between the sexes is made possible by the fact that we are male and female: "By God's will, man was not created alone but designed for the 'thou' of the other sex. The idea of man . . . finds its full meaning not in the male alone but in man and woman." [8]

Being human means that we have been made in the image of God. We bear his mark upon us. (See Gen. 1:26-27). The image is not something man bears by himself, nor is it something of woman alone. Rather it is the image borne by both man and woman.

God has made us human beings who are psycho-physical persons. There can be no divorce between body and spirit which are knit together in such a way that one is affected by the other. We do not have sex; we are sexual beings. The differentiation into male and female permeates our whole being. Sex is not limited to a physical function. It is wrapped up in the total being of a person. This does not mean that we should fit society's stereotypes about appropriate behavior for males and females. But sexual differentiation permeates our whole being. We are human beings of the male and female variety, and this difference dare not be obliterated. Sexual equality does not require that male and female be identical. True emancipation of the sexes enables us to be what God created us to be—human beings who are male and female. It is this human liberation which is our goal.

God is active as Creator and this has implications for our humanity. How will we respond to what he is doing in the world as Creator?

Responding to the Creator

God calls us to respond to his creative activity with celebration. Do not be ashamed of the fact that you are human! Celebrate your humanity, which is a good gift of God! The gone-wrongness in the world is not due to the fact that we are human but that we do not respond to God's call to be the humans we should be. We will examine this failure in the section on judgment which follows. Here we are interested in an affirmation of God's creation of humanity.

Not only should we be grateful that we are humans but that we are humans who are male or female. We are called to celebrate the maleness or the femaleness which permeates our human nature. Of course, society's cruel stereotypes about male and female should be rejected. But we must also reject the idea that all differences between males and females (other than anatomy) are culturally imposed differences.

In Christ, we are freed to be human. God calls males to celebrate their humanity, and this means for them to affirm the fact that they are males. God calls females to celebrate their humanity, and this means for them to affirm the fact that they are females.

There are many in women's liberation movements who can

learn a lesson from those who have participated in the liberation of black people. After being incorrectly taught that they should integrate with whites by trying to become white, blacks began to explore their uniqueness. They began to say, "Black is beautiful!" They began to affirm their own identity. This must happen in women's liberation movements as well. In response to the fact that God has made them what they are, women can say: "Woman is beautiful!" [9] Of course men have exploited beautiful women, and of course beautiful women have exploited men. The solution is not to try to obliterate beauty but to obliterate exploitation.

In addition to celebration, we can also respond to the Creator with a healthy stewardship of our humanity. Involved in this stewardship is the acceptance of self as a human being and respect for other human beings.

To be a good steward requires acceptance of our own humanity. We can learn what it means to be fully human by modeling our humanity after Jesus Christ. Acceptance of humanity requires acceptance of self as a sexual being. We are dependent to some extent upon parents, teachers, friends, and others to learn what it means to be fully human. This fact underscores the importance of a healthy interaction in the human community.

Stewardship of humanity also requires respect for other human beings. This means that we can show appreciation for God's creation by treating others as persons and not things. Males should show respect for females by acknowledging the common humanity which links them while also accepting the female's uniqueness. Females can demonstrate respect for males, although, of course, they should reject the continuing exploitation practiced by some males.

This response of respect also relates to sexual behavior: "Sexual relations which are motivated by purely selfish lust, without regard for the partner as a person, . . . carrying the image of a common creator, are like a two-edged sword dealing destruction on both sides." [10] The damage to the integrity of both sexes is the result of failure to respond to God's creative activity with respect for other sexual beings. A relational view of marriage calls for mutual respect between husband and wife. In a covenant of marriage two people meet each other as Thou rather than I. The husband shows respect for his wife when he treats her as a person who has a right to pleasure and satisfaction in intercourse. To treat her merely as a plaything to be used to satisfy the sexual appetite is a violation of her nature as a person whose sexuality is a part of her total being. At the same time, the wife turns her husband into an "it" when she uses him merely as an instrument to give her a child. Both husband and wife, therefore, are called to respond to God's creative activity by accepting each other as human beings to be respected and not as things to be used.

Active as Creator, God calls us to respond with celebration and stewardship. This is an essential part of any attempt to develop a theology of human liberation.

Judgment

God, who is acting in the world as Creator, also acts as Judge. Today some are reluctant to think of God as Judge, but this involves a serious misunderstanding of the nature and motivation of God's judgment. He judges not out of spite or malice, but to reject the work of sin and to bring about redemption. The implications of God's judgment will be explored here as they relate to a theology of human liberation.

God's Action as Judge

The Bible teaches that the Creator of everything is also the Judge. In Genesis the story of creation is followed immediately by the account of the Fall and God's consequent judgment upon Adam and Eve for their disobedience.

Two aspects of God's judgment appear in the biblical revelation: *control* and *condemnation*. God creates, and he sustains what he has made. He exercises control over his entire creation. He also condemns the misuse of his creation.

Misunderstanding about the nature of the Fall has contributed to the exploitation of women and the hostility between the sexes. Origen believed that the serpent seduced Eve in the Fall and physically infected her, thus making all sexual activity intrinsically wrong and the ground for all sins. Gregory of Nyssa taught that there was no sexual appetite before the Fall and that maleness and femaleness were a result of the Fall. If Adam and Eve had not sinned, according to Gregory, human propagation would have been patterned after that of the angels, perhaps by some type of fission.[11]

These ideas are extreme but they point to a tendency to attribute the Fall to sexual sin and to make Eve primarily responsible for most of the sin in the world. In truth, however, Genesis teaches that the Fall involves the failure of man and woman to be what God intended them to be. Estrangement between God and human beings is the result of self-assertion and the attempt to usurp God's sovereignty.

In the Garden, the serpent speaks to the woman first, not to the man. In the past men have explained why Eve was approached by speculating that she was weaker and more easily seduced.

Now women are beginning to speculate on this question. Phyllis Trible shows how to approach this question from a female point of view. She says maybe the "more subtle" serpent went to the woman because she is pictured in the biblical account as more intelligent, more aggressive, and one of greater sensibilities. Woman takes the initiative and eats the fruit without seeking the man's advice or permission. She is independent. But the man follows the woman in eating the fruit. He does not question, but silently acquiesces, Trible says, adding: "If the woman be intelligent, sensitive and ingenious, the man is passive, brutish and inept. Their character portrayals are truly extraordinary in a culture dominated by men. I stress their contrast not to promote female chauvinism but to undercut patriarchial interpretations alien to the text."[12]

The truth is that both male and female chauvinistic interpretations of the Fall must be rejected. We do not know why the serpent went to woman first in this account. But we do know that both sexes share in the sinfulness that characterizes humanity. We must reject the idea, therefore, that sexual differentiation is a result of the Fall. Humans are male or female because God created them this way. Sexual differentiation is a part of creation, not judgment. Here is a relevant word for all who see the sexes as a mistake.

What is the Fall all about? It is not about a woman using her sexual attractiveness to seduce an unwilling male to sin. It is not about a good, unisexual person being split into a sinful male and female. The Fall concerns instead the rebellion of two human beings who refused to be the fully human creatures God intended them to be. This is why liberation is needed.

Responding to God's Judgment

We are called to respond to God's judgment by acknowledging that it applies to us. We must accept this just condemnation of our failure to be fully human. It is easy for us to condemn others while ignoring our own sin. Some males must acknowledge their secret delight that society is so structured that they have an advantage over women in social institutions. Some females must confess to the sin of seeking to reverse the situation so that they have the favored position over males in society.

Not only must there be an acknowledgment of God's judgment but we must discipline ourselves to be fully human. Such discipline grows out of repentance for sin. And the discipline of self is in reality a gift from God which we can accept as we realize that God demands order in his creation.[13]

Some understand discipline to be the opposite of liberation. To be liberated is to be free from any shackles, including discipline, they say. This is not really the case. Indeed, the opposite is true. Discipline, properly exercised, gives us genuine liberation.

The misunderstanding of freedom is seen in a statement of

an atypical, radical liberation group called WITCH. (This acronym stands for several phrases: Woman's International Terrorists' Conspiracy from Hell; or Women Infuriated at Taking Care of Hoodlums; or Women Incensed at Telephone Company Harrassment; or Women Inspired to Commit Herstory)! This is called an "un-wedding" ceremony: "We are gathered together here in the spirit of our passion to affirm love and initiate our freedom from the unholy state of American patriarchial oppression. We promise to love, [and] cherish . . . all living things. We promise to smash the alienated family unit. We promise not to obey. . . . We promise these things until choice do us part. In the name of our sisters and brothers everywhere, and in the name of the Revolution, we pronounce ourselves Free Human Beings." [14] Nonsense!

We are also called to respond to the Judge by restraining the evil of sexual discrimination in society. E. Clinton Gardner states the case for this response: "We are forbidden to judge in holier-than-thou fashion; but we cannot remain neutral in the many social struggles of which we are a part by the very fact of our creation as social beings." [15] What we must do is respond to God by joining him to eliminate the discrimination against females (and where it exists, against males). To make society a place for humans to grow and to be free, we must work against those antihuman elements in our midst.

Having looked at some implications of creation and judgment for human liberation, we will now turn to God's activity as Redeemer.

Redemption

Although man and woman were created by God with freedom to be fully human, they rebelled and became enslaved by self-centeredness. The Creator has responded as Judge to control his creation and condemn the misuse of it. The fact that God also acts as Redeemer makes human liberation possible after all.

God's Action as Redeemer

God, who creates and judges, also redeems. By this action he moves to restore and deliver people who have been alienated from him. In other words, he provides a means by which we can be liberated and become what he intends us to be. God is actively seeking redemption in all events, but there is special significance in the life, death, and resurrection of Jesus Christ.

God liberates us by making possible through Christ reconciliation between the sexes: "There is neither Jew nor Greek, there is neither slave nor free, there is neither male nor female; for you are all one in Christ Jesus" (Gal. 3:28).

Now, some in the liberation movements dismiss Jesus as a liberator. Mary Daly, for example, in her book *Beyond God the Father* argues that women cannot make Jesus a model for liberation because he is a male savior who cannot possibly liberate women from patriarchal religion. She goes so far as to say that the "second coming is not a return of Christ but a new arrival of female presence, once strong and powerful but enchained since the dawn of patriarchy. . . . It is only female pride and self-affirmation that can release the memory of Jesus from its destructiveness and can *free* freedom to be *contagious.*" [16]

Such theologians as Mary Daly make the serious mistake of blaming Jesus for the exploitive excesses of some of his followers. Many feminists fail to recognize what Jesus has done and can do to liberate women and men as well. The revolutionary way in which Jesus treated women has been discussed in a thoughtful essay by Leonard Swidler in which he argues convincingly that "Jesus was a Feminist." [17]

It is not possible here to discuss in detail Jesus' actions in behalf of women, but several key points can be made. Jesus lived in a time when women were looked upon as inferior, yet Jesus treated them as humans with dignity. The rabbinic sayings of Jesus' time illustrate negative attitudes toward women: "It is well for those whose children are male, but ill for those whose children are female. . . . At the birth of a boy all are joyful, but at the birth of a girl all are sad. . . . When a boy comes into the world, peace comes into the world: when a girl comes, nothing comes. . . . Even the most virtuous of women is a witch. . . . Our teachers have said: Four qualities are evident in women: They are greedy at their food, eager to gossip, lazy and jealous." [18]

In such a setting, came Jesus the liberator. He taught women and commissioned them to bear witness of his resurrection even though the Judaic law forbade the bearing of witness by women. Further, he had disciples who were women at a time when women were not allowed to read or study. He also conversed with a Samaritan woman, thus violating tradition twice by talking to a Samaritan and to a woman. In the case of Mary and Martha (Luke 10:38-42), he recognized that women are not only to do household duty, but also to pursue an intellectual life as well. Indeed, in Luke 15 Jesus even compares God to a woman, who has lost a coin and then joyfully finds it. [19]

Jesus, therefore, treated women as persons and violated those traditions which dehumanized women. In doing this, he served as a model for human liberation. It was not only his life that benefited women but also his death and resurrection. Through these events, he made reconciliation between God and human beings possible. And he showed the way toward reconciliation between the sexes. It is through Jesus Christ, therefore, that true liberation is possible. Here is the good news which the Christian church must proclaim, especially at this time when so many are searching for liberation.

The redemptive activity of God gives us the proper light in which to understand woman. In Ephesians 5 she is seen as a type of the church. Her relation to her husband is like the relation of Christ to the church. As Dale Moody says, "This is a long way from an attitude of superiority on the part of man to subdue the woman and cast her aside for another when it suits his lusts better." [20]

Hope for a better society where exploitation and discrimination are no longer rampant is another implication of God's redemptive activity. Society will never be perfected, but giant strides can be taken toward justice as genuine community is made possible through Christ. Women's liberation movements cannot transform society; Jesus Christ alone can transform society. To say otherwise, as some in the liberation movements do, is to flirt with idolatry.[21]

The liberation available in Jesus Christ involves the expression of love which he has demonstrated in his life for others. His is a giving love which enables man and woman to be fully human. In this regard, Karl Braaten argues that it is not enough to seek justice in society for men and women; we must also seek love: "The quest for liberation not carefully guided by the demands of love in its multi-dimensional reality will only lead to new forms of alienation and oppression. . . . Women's power can bring justice as it is doing in all fields, but only love can bring liberation." [22]

Responding to God's Redemptive Activity

How can we respond to what God is doing in the world to liberate us as human beings? In our relations with all people we can express love. There are some in the women's liberation movements who are reluctant to urge women to be loving toward men because they fear that this would put women in the same sacrificial attitude into which they have been forced for so many years. What we must seek instead is a fully human love on the part of men and women. It would be sinister, indeed, for men to advocate that women practice love simply to keep women from being a problem. Thus, love and justice must be linked. As Sidney Callahan says: "I think love and education, soul force and truth force are the only means which will work in the long run. Loving one's enemies and oppressors keeps one from imitating them and falling into their same errors. We want women to become aggressive in the good sense, not in the destructive aggressive way that men have adopted. Besides, it takes more strength to be peaceful; you can't keep turning your own inadequacies into aggression against some enemy out there." [23]

Although love affects all human relationships, we will focus on the love expressed between mates here. After all, marriage is not—let it be repeated—not required for a person to be fully human. But married people do need to look at ways they can express love toward each other to enhance their full humanity.

Since some caught up in women's liberation movements have found their marriages breaking up, it is good to take a look at the response of love between mates. We will examine three aspects of love designated by *eros, philia,* and *agape.*

Eros aims at the possession and enjoyment of the objective value of another. It is not limited to sexual behavior, although this can be an important aspect of *eros.* It includes *libido* (desire for sexual union) but goes beyond it to erotic fascination with the sheer loveliness of another.[24] Disappointment with marriages based on *eros* has led many to believe that marriage is to be rejected as unworkable. No doubt the romantic love cult in America has contributed to such a delusion about marriage. *Eros* is essential in a healthy marriage, but it is not enough.

There must also be *philia* in marriage—the love of friendship. As a matter of fact, *philia* is a trait which should characterize relations of males and females at work, in social settings, in classrooms, and elsewhere. But a suspiciousness by some neo-Puritans that all friendships must lead to bed has kept the sexes apart. Hopefully, wholesome *philia* will increasingly characterize male-female relationships.

Philia means that a husband and wife can also be friends. If a couple is able to bring companionship and a life of shared interests and aspirations to intercourse, they will find a satisfaction that will last after their passion has subsided.

Philia is impossible as long as women look at men as the enemy. *Philia* is impossible as long as men look at women as a target for a potential sexual score. What is needed is greater sharing between husband and wife in their life-styles, because as Braaten says, "We have reason to worry when models of liberation are advanced that draw husbands and wives into completely different life-situations." [25]

The egoism of *eros* and *philia* can be transformed by *agape*. This love is not an emotion or a feeling, but an act of will. *Agape* is not selfish. It seeks what is best for another human as a child of God, and it stands against exploitation in and outside the covenant of marriage. God acts as Redeemer, therefore, to demonstrate the meaning of *agape* in the self-giving of Christ and offers his love as a gift through the Holy Spirit (Gal. 5:28). Those who do not incorporate this self-giving love in their sexual relationships will not discover the lasting fulfillment they really need for genuine happiness.

Closely related and including love is another response to the Redeemer, namely sharing in community. In regard to human liberation, we can best do this by sharing in the church, which is a community of hope.

Mary Daly calls for sisterhood which will be a genuine community of sharing unlike the unequal sharing of the "brotherhoods" of the past. She is correct in denouncing the discrimination of many so-called brotherhoods, but wrong in her views that the sisterhood must, therefore, be anti-church. [26]

Although the church has not lived up to Christ's intentions, it is still our best hope for a community of truly liberated human beings. The church can offer encouragement to those who despair over the possibility of genuine liberation of males and females to live together in responsible relationships.

Women are going to be free! God requires it. Justice demands it. Our Constitution guarantees it. And many Christian women and men are going to keep working under the leadership of the Holy Spirit to help churches reflect God's intention that all humans be free.

Freedom for women is a powerful idea whose time has come. Indeed, the idea that all human beings can be free came with Jesus Christ. This idea will not go away. Extremists in women's liberation movements cannot kill it with their clever and yet unfeeling rhetoric. It cannot be killed by women who want to stay in their male-imposed places so they will not have to face the risk of freedom. Male arrogance cannot kill it. Female indifference cannot kill it. It is Christ's idea and it is here to stay. Consciousness must yet be raised and skirmishes will have to be fought, but women are going to be free. Women are not second class citizens in God's kingdom, and they must not be second class citizens in religious institutions. The church can be a model for this kind of relationship for the rest of society. Some church fellowships are already doing this, and we must call on others to follow Christ all the way to such a society of fully liberated human beings.

Notes

1. Margaret N. Maxey, "Beyond Eve and Mary," *Dialog*, X (Spring, 1971), 116.

2. Harvey Cox, "Eight Theses on Female Liberation," *Christianity and Crisis* (October 4, 1971), p. 199.

3. This approach of God's activity and man's response has been developed in the works of H. Richard Niebuhr and by his students, E. Clinton Gardner and Waldo Beech.

4. Phyllis Trible, "Good Tidings of Great Joy: Biblical Faith Without Sexism," *Christianity and Crisis*, (February 4, 1974), 13.

5. *Ibid.*

6. A Guillaumont *et al.* (trans.), *The Gospel According to Thomas* (New York: Harper and Brothers, 1959), p. 57.

7. Georgia Harkness, *Woman in Church and Society* (Nashville: Abingdon Press, 1972), p. 187.

8. Gerhard von Rad, *Genesis* (Philadelphia: Westminster Press, 1961), p. 58.

9. See Karl Braaten, "Untimely Reflections on Women's Liberation," *Dialog* (Spring, 1971), 106.

10. William Graham Cole, *Sex in Christianity and Psychoanalysis* (New York: Harper and Row, 1952), p. 297.

11. See Norman Powell Williams, *The Ideas of the Fall and of Original Sin* (London: Longmans, Green and Company, 1927), p. 271.

12. *Ibid.*

13. See 2 Timothy 1:7: "For God did not give us a spirit of timidity but a spirit of power and love and self-control."

14. Quoted in *Sisterhood Is Powerful*, edited by Robin Morgan (New York: Random House, 1970), pp. 546-47.

15. E. Clinton Gardner, *Biblical Faith and Social Ethics* (New York: Harper and Brothers, 1960), p. 169.

16. Mary Daly, *Beyond God the Father* (Boston: Beacon Press, 1973), p. 96.

17. Leonard Swidler, "Jesus Was a Feminist," CCXII, *Catholic World* (January, 1971), pp. 177-83.

18. *Ibid.*, pp. 178-79.

19. *Ibid.*, pp. 180, 183.

20. Dale Moody, *Baptist Courier* (July 17, 1973), p. 4.

21. James Hitchcock, "Women's Liberation: Tending Toward Idolatry," *Christian Century* (Sept. 22, 1961), p. 1106.

22. Braaten, *op. cit.,* p. 108.

23. Sidney Callahan, "A Christian Perspective on Feminism," *Women's Liberation and the Church,* ed. by Sarah Bentley Doley (New York: Association Press, 1970), p. 45.

24. Braaten, *op. cit.,* p. 107.

25. *Ibid.,* p. 107.

26. Daly, *op. cit.,* pp. 132 ff.

4
Women and the Family in Christian History

Vera and David Mace

In chapter 1 we explored the position of women in the Bible. This is territory where we all feel free to have ideas and theories, whether we are simple Christians or studious ones. Because we are able to read the Bible in our own language, though this is not the one in which it was first recorded, we have become familiar with life as we think it was lived then, and we get support and comfort from the direct link that this provides us between today's living and that of Bible times.

We have no such single link between modern times and the Christian history which we will now consider. There must be thousands of different books in many different languages which record significant aspects of the Christian history of the position and life of women, both inside and outside the family. Some of these we have read, and we have used the sources they unfold to paint the picture we want to present to you. However, we cannot point to any one written work and say, "read that, and you'll understand all." Instead, we must try to paint a picture in very broad strokes because it must cover at least nineteen hundred years and deal with a factor in human life as universal as human life itself—the way women lived during those years.

In ancient times the world was believed to be much, much smaller than we know it to be today. The hint of a mysterious world in the Far East concerned hardly anyone, and the possibility of a Western continent with human beings living on it was utterly remote. The world of early Christian history centered in the lands around the Mediterranean Sea—the very name of which means "the middle of the earth." From there the passing of history brought the spread of Christianity to lands further

and further from the "Middle Sea"—a process which is still
going on in our own day.

Granted that the limits of the known world were narrow and
confined compared with what we now know, how much more
circumscribed were the lives of everyday people compared with
our lives today? It is hard for us to imagine living in a world
where ordinary people never went more than a few miles from
the place where they were born and knew nothing of what was
going on beyond their village or community unless some in-
trepid traveller happened to pass by and bring news which
generally was too strange to be believed. It was of course a
world without telephones, TV, radios, and the like. It is perhaps
not so hard to imagine a world where families grew their own
food, and had to eat only what they harvested from the land
and sea themselves and prepared with their own hands—no
packaged, or prepared, or processed foods. What did those
people, the ordinary people, wear? What the family—mostly
the women—could spin and weave by hand, and then sew into
garments—no weaving or sewing machines, no drip-dry fabrics,
no ready-made clothes. Was there any leisure in that world?
Probably very little, particularly for women, and such as there
was had to provide home-made entertainment—mainly through
music in its many forms and through the telling of stories.

The Period of the Early Church

Our chapter on "Women and the Family in the Bible" led
us to see how, through the respect he showed women, through
the relationships he had with women, and through his demonstration of his new way of thinking about women, Jesus elevated
womanhood to a height it had never before attained. In the
light of the standards of his day, this was startlingly revolutionary, "a momentous change"—a complete turning around.

We saw how these first Christians, and especially Paul, firmly
believed in what was called "the Parousia"—the return of Christ
to establish his kingdom on earth—and how the effect of this
belief on everyday living tended at first to make Christians

unconcerned about the regulation of ordinary affairs, in order to prepare themselves for a new kind of near-divine existence. When the expected Parousia did not take place as they thought it would, there was an inevitable lowering of standards and slipping back into some pre-Christian practices in relation to the position and treatment of women.

In addition to this, as more and more converts who had not known Jesus or his early followers were accepting the new faith, a bewildering variety of ideas about women and their place in Christianity, in the society of the day, and in the family had to be woven into some kind of acceptable and functioning pattern. For example, on the one hand there were those who taught that marriage was utterly wicked and that no new convert to Christianity should marry. Those who were already married and wished to become Christians should be required to dissolve the tie. Relationships between men and women, if already married, should be only on a "spiritual" level, never on a physical one. On the other hand, some taught that human laws, for example those to regulate marriage, were violating divine laws and as such were neither just nor necessary. "The desires we have by nature are our rights, on which no human institution may set limits." Unfortunately the desires mankind had "by nature" led to unbridled license. Most regrettable of all was that in all this wrangling and argument about the position of women, the teachings of Jesus and the demonstrations of his life were mostly forgotten, or if remembered at all, ignored. It was out of this raw material, often very raw, that the first Christian church had to be fashioned and built.

The primary work of the early church was to formulate Christian doctrine in order that the faith could be established and maintained in the face of external opposition and internal heresy. This was a colossal task, and we cannot judge its magnitude by comparing it with the relatively insignificant, but to us highly important, struggles within the church of today in the formulation of policies and procedures. It may seem a little strange to us that the position of women needed to be regulated by doctrine, but we must remember that doctrine means "What is taught as a body of principles." There was great need for a definition of what should be taught and recognized about women. Before Christ there were many evidences of woman being treated as a goddess—a mysterious being, whose function as the producer of new life demanded that she be appeased or even worshipped. These early makers of doctrine—all men—had to get women into a theological context which would satisfy their need to silence heresy and give some kind of answer to their personal questions about women.

The first thing they decided was that woman brought sin and death into the world through Eve's disobedience in the Garden of Eden. Here is how Tertullian, who lived a hundred, to a hundred and fifty years after Christ, speaking to all Christian women, expressed it:

Do you know that you are each an Eve? The sentence of God on this sex of yours lives in this age; the guilt must of necessity live too. You are the devil's gateway; you are the unsealer of that forbidden tree; you are the first deserter of the divine law; you are she who persuaded him whom the devil was not valiant enough to attack. You destroyed so easily God's image—man. On account of your desert . . . even the Son of God had to die.

These beliefs and ideas continued on in various forms for hundreds of years. Jerome, another theologian of the early church, declared that the only good thing that could be said for a married woman was that she might rise to be called *Socrus Dei*. Literally translated this means the "mother-in-law of God"; that is, the mother of a child who would become wedded to the church.

Not satisfied with trying to determine woman's position in general society, these early theologians invaded her personal life by trying to impose controls on what woman should wear. Clement of Alexandria, who died about the year 215, wrote about woman's dress—particularly for going to church: "Let her be entirely covered, unless she happens to be at home.

For that style of dress is grave, and protects from being gazed at—she will never fall who puts before her face modesty and her shawl; nor will she invite another to fall into sin by uncovering her face."

When we think of how much is "uncovered" today, we cannot refrain from saying women have come a long way since the days of the early church! Those early fathers even had views on cosmetics for women which Cyprian called pollution "by adulterous colors," which changed what was true into a lie by the use of "deceitful dyes of medicaments."

Even if a woman had what the theologians called "natural grace," she was enjoined by Tertullian to obliterate it "by concealment and negligence, as being dangerous to the glance of the beholders' eyes." And Cyprian summed it up thus: "Let your countenance remain in you incorrupt, your head unadorned, your figure simple; let not wounds be made in your ears, nor let the precious chain of braclets and necklaces circle your arms or your neck; let your feet be free from golden bands, your hair stained with no dye, your eyes worthy of beholding God."

Underlying these attempts on the part of the early church leaders to control the lives of women we see clearly a loathing of physical sex and a mortal dread that any involvement with it would contaminate them and condemn them to eternal damnation. It is hardly surprising that this false asceticism, and the loathing of sex resulting from it, were quickly blamed on women, whom the leaders of the church saw to be the cause of all the trouble, the origin of temptation, and the sirens luring men to their downfall.

Some of the early Christian leaders went to incredible lengths to protect themselves from the snares of women. Complete separation seemed to some to be the only way—hence they went to live as hermits in desert caves and cells. Others sought to make themselves inaccessible by living on the tops of high pillars. the most famous of these was Simon Stylites, who lived on a small platform on the top of a high pillar for more than thirty-five years—to stay away from women!

This fear of the potential power of woman over man extended beyond her reproductive years—if she survived that long. Thus, they came to believe that there was something exceptional and unusual about an old woman which had to be explained (by men). What better explanation could there be than that such a woman had a peculiar association with the devil? We shall return to this belief later in our chronological survey.

Clearly, for the good of mankind, women must be kept under the very tight and complete control of men. Not only the faith, but the law also required this, so in the early Christian centuries we find the girl "belonged" utterly and completely to her father until she married, to her husband when she married, and to her son or sons after she was widowed. The fact that these controls were sometimes benign rather than tyrannical did nothing to mitigate the humiliation they imposed.

During the first two to three hundred years of Christianity there came into existence the idea that celibacy was more virtuous than marriage, and that virginity, for both men and women, though particularly for men, was the highest and the most exclusive Christian virtue. Cyprian wrote: "Virgins are the flower of the ecclesiastical tree—a joyful race—the image of God's holiness—the most illustrious portion of Christ's flock." Athenagoras said: "Many among us, both men and women, have grown old in a state of celibacy through the hope that they shall thereby be more closely united to God." This seems to have been an expression of a genuine desire for holiness, but it left the newly emerging church faced with a dilemma— what to do about marriage. If all Christians maintained celibacy, how would the faith, and the race, be continued? Obviously such denial was an entirely untenable position which would have resulted finally in complete annihilation. Some of the church fathers tried to have the best of both sides of the issue, as is revealed in Jerome's famous saying—"I praise marriage, I praise wedlock, but (only) because they bear me virgins. I gather from the thorn the rose, from the earth the gold, from the shell the pearl." A more realistic attitude to the dilemma came from Ambrose who lived 339 (?)–397. He claimed that, although virginity was the quickest way of salvation, the way of matrimony might also lead there ultimately.

As the first phase of our Christian history was drawing to a close, do we have a picture of what the life of woman, in marriage, was like at that time? We know that Tertullian, who constantly elevated celibacy, was nonetheless able, when speaking to heretics who condemned marriage altogether, to say that marriage was a pure and honorable estate. John Langdon-Davies in his book, *A Short History of Women* quotes an unnamed first-century Christian writer:

He that desires a chaste wife lives chastely, pays her conjugal duties, eats with her, lives with her, comes with her to be sanctified by the preacher, does not grieve her or find fault with her unreasonably, seeks to please her, and procure her all the pleasures in his power, and makes up for what he cannot give her with caresses. Not that the chaste wife requires these caresses to do her duty. She looks on her husband as her master. If he be poor, she bears with his poverty; she hungers with him if he be hungry. If he go to a foreign land, she goes with him. She consoles him when he is sad—the prudent woman is temperate in her eating or drinking. She never remains alone with young men, she even avoids old men, and she shuns unseemly mirth. She takes pleasure in grave discourse and flies from all that is not decorous.

The Middle Ages

We have given more space to the early church period than we can give to the Middle Ages, or to the Reformation and Post-Reformation Period, because it is in the early stages that the roots of so much later blossoming are to be found. For example, what were the developments from those early ideas of celibacy about which we have just talked? Because the church began to think of marriage as impure at its lowest evaluation, and only a second-best at its highest, it followed naturally that the church's chief servants, its clergy, should be expected to live at the higher level and be denied marriage. This had definitely not been true in the days of the first Christians—a woman could then be the wife of a priest, provided she was not a widow when she married him—that would have been unlawful. But then the situation started to change, and, in the great Church Council of Nicea in the year 325, an attempt was made to enforce the celibacy of the priesthood, and to compel any who had been ordained before that date to refrain, as a duty, from cohabiting with their wives. This was only rejected following the earnest advice of the saintly Paphnutius, who pleaded for the sanctity of marriage, although he himself was a strict celibate. However, by the end of that century, some seventy-five years later, the celibacy of the clergy was universally adopted as law in Western Christendom. By that time, the Christian church had split into the Roman Catholic section and the Eastern Orthodox section. In the Eastern Church the celibacy of the priesthood was not enforced on any of the lower orders of the clergy. Those married before ordination were allowed to continue in the state of matrimony, except in the case of a bishop. The wife of a bishop had either to become a deaconess or enter a convent.

This struggle to impose celibacy on its priests continued within the Church for hundreds of years—throughout the times we are now considering. An early Pope during this period, Gregory the Great (c. 540-604), thought of the clergy as "Soldiers of a spiritual army—not to be fathers, husbands and citizens like everyone else, but citizens of the 'Civitas Dei' (God's Kingdom) bound by ties of absolute military obedience to their supreme commander, the Pope." This led a later logician to remark that marriage was ordained by Christ; celibacy was ordered by the Papacy—therefore as Christ was greater than the Pope, marriage was greater than celibacy. The anomaly involved was highlighted when, years later, the Chruch elevated marriage to become one of its seven sacred sacraments but continued to deny it to the highest servants and representatives of the same Church—the clergy. Thus, a holy sacrament was denied to the

Church's highest members.

From the deep roots of sacerdotal celibacy there flowered through the Middle Ages that sturdy growth known as monasticism. This was the arrangement whereby those who felt a call to a fully religious kind of life renounced the pursuit of ordinary daily living and went instead to live in religious communities set apart from common and ordinary mortals, where they could glorify God with praise and prayer, and with whatever labors they felt would contribute to their relationship with him. In this way they would avoid the contamination of the sinful world and of what they thought to be its depraved ways. This holy call could come to women as well as to men, and it enabled many of them to achieve levels of personal development denied to them otherwise.

At first these communities gave shining examples of noble living which, as well as providing leadership in the faith, included service to mankind through the ministries of teaching and healing. It is sad to have to relate that with more power, more influence, and more wealth, the cancer of corruption set in, and depravities which were legion sullied the original idealistic dreams of the founders of the movement and made a travesty of the teachings of Jesus, particularly about relationships between men and women. In the long patience of God's time, there came new visionaries who established orders which rose above this festering corruption. Among these was Francis of Assisi who, along with his followers (the men called Franciscans and the women Poor Clares) embraced not only chastity but also poverty. Francis was able to rekindle, by example as well as teaching, a more Christ-like form of ministering to mankind.

In the meantime, while a relatively small number of women chose the religious life, women generally lived in a number of clearly recognizable patterns, two of which we shall examine briefly.

The high-born women of the various Christian lands. Though most of these must have lived in comparative luxury and ease, some showed sincere and deep identification with noble Christian ideals and practices. They dispensed justice and charity, insofar as they had opportunity and power, and some few of them had a great deal, being rulers of lands in their own right. This was an age when Christian men went to fight holy wars against the infidel, and between the eleventh and thirteenth centuries some high-born women accompanied their husbands on the Crusades. they travelled in leisurely fashion with vast entourages across Europe to the Holy Land. They took their luxuries with them and would seem almost to have enjoyed these pseudo-heroic journeyings. But in an age when the subjection of women by the church was being firmly maintained, we find here the seed of a Christian independence among women who were not professional *religieuses,* but who were determined to be involved in whatever ways they could with what was going on in the Christian world in which they lived.

The peasant or low-born women of Christian lands. These were at the farthest extreme from those we have just described. For them, day followed day, bringing hard and long hours of domestic work within the homes of their overlord and his family, as well as in their own poor living quarters. Outdoors, with other members of their own families, they shared in the struggle to produce sufficient food and sustenance to augment the meager rations provided by their employers, who were in fact the owners and controllers of their lives. Poverty and hard work protected them from the temptations of luxury and ease. Their misfortune was that they had too much labor and too much protection; yet through their simplicity of living they could draw nearer to the fountain source of Christianity and to the one who came to bring release to the over-burdened. In an age of increasingly manifest corruption and decay, it was in the hearts and lives of such simple women that the torch of the Christian faith was preserved and kept alive. The challenge with which Christ had confronted woman had not died or diminished—it was biding its time in readiness for a new flowering.

Before we leave the Middle Ages there is one aspect of the

lives of women to which we must give consideration. We have already referred to the fact that in early Christian times some women were believed to be under the control of the devil. During the Middle Ages these beliefs became centered in the idea, not by any means a new one historically, that such women were witches—possible incarnations of the devil himself. Some church leaders felt that the presence of these women in the Christian world demanded rigorous persecution by the Church. This was started in the Middle Ages, though it did not reach its height until a later period. At first, such persecution was not notably violent, but there is no doubt that, in time, religious persecution led to frightful torture and horrifying forms of death. Many innocent, but ignorant and harmless, women suffered untold misery and pain as a result of being falsely accused as witches. And all this in the name of the followers of Christ!

The Reformation and Since

This last period brings us much closer to our own day even though what is known as the Reformation—the great cleansing and reform of the Christian church—started over 450 years ago. This is because until the very recent past, Christian men and women have lived within the scope of many of the direct results of the Reformation.

We are conscious of the fact that, in this survey, we have so often had to seek information about the lives of women through the pronouncements of men about women or through descriptions of what men thought about women and how they treated women. This is a clear reflection of the state of subjection and inferiority to which women in general were relegated. Although the beliefs and practices of the Church were truly purified and reformed by the Reformation and women did derive indirect benefits, their position as inferior Christian citizens remained virtually unchanged, at least until the twentieth century; and some of our contemporaries would claim that they are still unchanged today.

It is in the area of reforms about marriage that we see the greatest effect of the Reformation in the lives of women. The degenerate condition of the priesthood at the time of the Reformation frequently meant that priests, in spite of their vows of celibacy, were actually living in sin, as one historian described it, "overburdened with women and children" and very often deeply troubled by their consciences over this state of affairs. Luther, the foremost leader of the Reformation, had in 1505 joined the order of Augustinian monks and made, along with his other monastic vows, a solemn renunciation of marriage. Fourteen years later he was led of God to challenge the whole system of monastic vows. In his famous sermon doing this, he described marriage as, "Truly a noble, great and blessed state—if it be rightly observed." He conceded that popes and bishops might be required of God to make and maintain vows of celibacy, but he claimed that their situation was essentially different from that of those parish priests who were required by the nature of their pastoral office to live among the rank and file of mankind and minister to their common needs. Here he felt it was necessary for them to be able, if they so desired, to live "an ordinary domestic life." It must, however, be pointed out that the throwing off of the compulsion to celibacy should not involve a man in taking on the opposite compulsion, that of being forced to marry. Luther felt that the question of whether a man, be he priest or not, should marry was one which each person must decide for himself in relation to his understanding of God's will for him. This, of course, applied to women too.

For the expression of these views Luther was excommunicated by the Church and was only saved from the usual fate of a heretic by being forcibly abducted by his friends and carried off into exile. At this time Luther himself had no intention of marrying, but shortly after this he became involved in collecting funds for the support of nine nuns who had escaped from their convent, though he had not been involved in the actual escape. One of these women was Catherine von Bora, who, at twenty-four years of age, had spent fourteen years in a convent, under her vow of celibacy. Luther was married to Catherine, the ex-nun, on June 13, 1525. The ceremony was almost secret, as Luther took none of his friends into his confidence.

"It is not good," he said, "to talk much about such matters. A man must ask God for counsel, and pray, and then act accordingly."

As one would have expected, Luther's marriage was the occasion of tremendous criticism. A letter his friend Melanchton wrote three days after the wedding to another friend is a very revealing mixture of his annoyance and loyalty:

You will perhaps wonder that in this unhappy time, while good and right-minded men are everywhere sore distressed, he does not sorrow with them, but rather it seems, lives voluptously and tarnishes his reputation, when Germany specially needs his wisdom and strength—the nuns fell upon him and plotted against him with their wiles.

The old story—marriage is voluptuous, and if Luther had succumbed it must have been woman, in the shape of the escaped nun, who lured him into it by her wicked wiles! However, Melancthon, struggling not to reject Luther, continues:

I write thus that you may not be troubled overmuch by the incredible affair. For I know you care for Luther's reputation and regret to see it lowered. I exhort you to take the matter calmly, for in the Holy Scripture marriage is said to be honourable, and to many is probably a necessity.

When the criticism and censure died down, the reformers came, in time, to experience marriage as a blessing and a means of mutual helpfulness and to find in their wives the "helpmeet" that God had promised woman might be to man.

Though the Reformation did not emancipate women nor destroy the superstitions and tyrannies of former centuries, it did give them enhanced status, and it fostered and nurtured the seed which would grow into a new freedom for Christian women—a freedom to be themselves and to seek directly God's purpose for their lives without having to be dependent upon the directions and interpretations of men. A few more centuries were still to pass, however, before the issue of the woman's right to full personhood would become a challenge so insistent that the church would have to confront it and settle it.

5
A History of Women's Liberation Movements

Sarah Frances Anders

The liberation of women has taken as many forms as there have been types of oppressive actions against them. The historical treatment of attempts to free women from the recurring cultural patterns of subordination and oppression, however, must use the vocabulary of the current movements, if it would give unity and continuity to the struggle. It cannot be seen simply as a struggle for certain categorical "rights," though it assuredly is this; it must be viewed as inherently a movement for the total recognition of women as persons of worth, deserving equal status and opportunity with men. It strives for recognition meted to all according to their unique talents, skills, and education.

Intrinsic to such a movement is the fact that biological differences between the sexes are neither disdained nor denied. Rather, the dichotomy of male-female is second only to that of creator-created among living beings.[1] The Christian views the liberation of women as being theologically sound, based on the essential equality of creaturehood, the more so of human creatures who share the distinction of being "made in the image of the creator." There are biological distinctives among all creatures; some swim better, some fly higher, others run more speedily, and many breed more rapidly. None of these attributes justifies labeling the total behavior of any species as superior or inferior.

"Sexism" then is a fundamental concept in the vocabulary of the movers in current liberation groups. It refers to the belief that one sex group is innately superior to the other and thus has the right to dominate the inferior one. Emerging from the implications of this mental set is the polar concept of "feminism." This may be defined as the conviction that women must have equal political, economic, social, and spiritual rights to men. It also refers to any movements which accept this premise and seek to obtain these rights.

Feminists and feminism are often difficult to separate, for it is always difficult to differentiate dramatic "movers" and their contemporary movements. The Christian, in viewing history, seeks to give dignity to both movers and movements in such a cause, for they are persons of innate worth, whether singularly or collectively, whether we can accept their goals and methods or not. We cannot fall prey to the kind of ridicule and humor some critics project toward the contemporary movements. The surge to emancipate womankind is no more a joke than movements to liberate the Mexican truck farmer, the forgotten Indian, an unsaved Jew, or the caste black. Such failure to take feminism seriously blunts both the efforts and the inherent values of the movement, as well as the Christian perspective.

Women in Early Civilizations

Just at what point in antiquity woman fell into subservience to man is hard to determine. Was Eve's action in the blissful primeval life more than a sign of defiance against divine authority? Or was it also a foreboding of the wiles she would use perennially on man to assert some sort of control over the course of human events? Some today would like to dwell only on current revolution without understanding that the seeds of the now-culture were in the then-centuries.

Anthropological evidence suggests that in more than one primitive society, family groups appeared maternal, if not matriarchal. But as L. T. Hobhouse has declared in his classic *Morals in Evolution*,[2] never was there absolute authority vested in woman. It was instead a matrilineal pattern of inheritance in which daughters were under their fathers and brothers, rather than their husbands. Only a relatively short span of history lapsed before women became subordinate to their husbands, however, and both women and children were included among the properties of the husband and father. This was the cultural heritage of modern Judaism. It was a life-style in which sex probably exceeded age differences as a basis for differential and discriminatory treatment. Only among the ancient Egyptians were some women, who were born to wealth or nobility, permitted to attain a measure of power and prestige.

The ancient Greeks and Romans more readily gave privilege and power to women in their mythology than in everyday social experience. Who can doubt this in the legends surrounding Juno, wife of Jupiter; Minerva, the goddess of wisdom; Venus, the goddess of love and beauty; Ceres, the goddess of earth and agriculture; or Diana, the goddess of the hunt? Two classes of Greek women emerged: the sheltered, faithful, pure, married woman and the hetaerae, who were highly skilled entertainers and courtesans, moving freely and conspicuously among men in public places. Doubtless, it was against such behavior permitted the hetaerae that Paul spoke to the Corinthian women (1 Cor. 14:34-35). He feared Christian women would be mistaken for hetaerae if they were too free in dress and speech.

Even the Greek philosophers did not agree on the status of women. Plato advocated complete sex equality in his ideal republic, where women would be educated, go to battle, and hold high office along with men. But Aristotle saw women as basically inferior, at their best in childbearing and childrearing.[3]

Women in the New Testament and Early Church Periods

The teachings of Jesus provide an ethical system, based on two systems of interpersonal relationships: between creator/parent and creature/child, between person and person. He dealt with broad principles rather than narrow particulars; so, we have no separate Christian ethic for blacks, national presidents, wetbacks, or Biafrans any more than there is an ethic dealing with the treatment of women. Jesus' actions, however, were a series of enlightening particulars, in the warmth of his personal relations with women and in the respect and tenderness he showed them. Whatever the distinctions he made between the twelve disciples, who happened to be male, and his intimate associates, who included a number of women, they were not the basis for a hierarchy of sexes. He provided the premise and the seeds for liberation.

The first-century apostles and writers, who traveled further than Jesus and were more affected by Eastern tradition, often launched out beyond principles to utter minute exhortations concerning dress, hair, jewelry, conversation, and public behavior. This did not prevent key women, who were scattered abroad, such as Priscilla, Dorcas, and Lydia, from being leaders in the church. These women were liberated, whether in the fullest social context or not, for they were business women, free to move, to speak, and to lead.

The Intervening Eighteen Centuries

What little freedom and measure of equality were provided women in certain pre-Christian societies was enhanced by the affirming example of Jesus. The early church fathers eventually returned to a pre-Christian position regarding women. Canon law, more and more, abrogated the equality exemplified by Jesus and reinforced the total subjection of women through restricting and discriminating judgments which concerned marriage, divorce, adultery, guardianship of children, and rape. In practice, it permitted a vicious double standard for at least men of means and nobility to enjoy.[4] The only liberation movement that was apparent in the middle centuries was the growth of conventual groups that gave women the right to choose something other than marriage, numerous children, and subjection to the will of man. Here was the opportunity to choose God over husband; the convent offered a voluntary servitude that brought status and opportunity for personhood not possible anywhere else in that culture.

The Early Modern Period

Many current members of the liberation front trace the roots of the contemporary movement back to these very early periods of oppression, and they record the feeble attempts of women to assert themselves culturally as almost a trail of blood and tears. The Renaissance and Reformation were to be both a bane and a blessing to women. It was a setback in that Protestantism cut off many of the monastic opportunities for education and service. The advances came through a few groups such as Quakers and Baptists who, less encumbered with ecclesiastical trappings, allowed some women to serve and to preach. Like Elizabeth Fry, an English, Quaker preacher who led out in prison reform, they would help the gospel turn the world upside down for many of the rejects of society.

In England, where single and widowed women had minimal property and guardianship rights, the emerging factory system produced less sense of personal dignity for most workers, but particularly for women. No one spoke nor wrote more dramatically for the worth of persons and the equality of the sexes in England during this period than John Stuart Mill, member of Parliament and early philosopher of science. Indeed, William Robert Carr has called Mill's *The Subjection of Women*, published in 1869, "the most eloquent and ambitious plea in the English language for equality of the sexes." [5] Carr considers it to be an entire scheme of social ethics in four short chapters. But these concise premises, virtually a secular sermon, have provided the philosophical basis, which a hundred years later still is unchallenged but rather exalted for the intellectual monument of the current women's liberation movement. Mill's arguments were based on the social-psychological assertion that masculine and feminine natures did not differ fundamentally.

In Colonial America, the scarcity of women and the rigors of pioneer life had brought some property rights and esteem to women which were diminished by early industrialism. But the seeds of feminism were there in the letters of Abigail Adams, wife of one president and mother of another, as she admonished her husband while he was at the Constitutional Convention in 1777, "I desire you would remember the ladies and be more generous and favorable to them than your ancestors . . . If Particular care and attention is not paid to the ladies, we are determined to foment a rebellion, and will not hold ourselves bound by any laws in which we have no voice or representation." [6]

Women "with Cause"

Abigail Adams may not have organized "to foment," but a movement was already underway which would provide the vehicle basic to many crusades for liberation of others and of women. It was the great quest for freedom through education. The women who pioneered for female seminaries and later for female colleges were inevitably to contribute directly or indirectly to two other great movements: abolitionism and suffragism. At least forty women's colleges that had their origins over a century ago and persist today taught young women not only how to excel in certain female skills, but to be adept in literature, history, mathematics, and geography—the masculine subjects! So they were a vital part of the social climate that would breed movements capable of radical challenge to the assumption of female subordination.

Education enabled some individual women to pioneer in public life, decades before they would be organized to effect national changes. One of the most charming and magnetic speakers for women's rights was also the first woman known to maintain her maiden name for public life, Lucy Stone Blackwell. She was friend, college roommate, and sister-in-law to Antoinette Brown Blackwell, who became the first ordained woman in America (September 15, 1853) and pastored a Congregational church in New York. As early as 1835 a woman was practicing medicine; Elizabeth Blackwell and her sister Emily, along with Harriot Hunt, shared the honors of being the first American women doctors. The public was somewhat accustomed to the idea of women doctors when Miss Ada Kepley and Mrs. Arabella Mansfield began to practice law about 1870, but Mrs. Belva Lockwood was the first woman to present a case before the United States Supreme Court in 1878. Women like Sarah J. Hale and Lydia Maria Child were receiving literary recognition for some time before women's rights literature appeared.[7] Mrs. Phebe A. Hanaford, a Universalist minister who pastored three churches, authored a dozen books, led in her denomination, and was chaplain of the Connecticut Legislature, included 973 biographical sketches of eminent women of the first century of the American republic in one of her remarkable books. Women scientists, artists, reformers, doctors, journalists, missionaries, and business leaders were among the twenty-six categories included.[8]

The early movements which involved women's rights fall into three periods that span much of the nineteenth century and the first two decades of the twentieth. The first period began with the visit of the Scotswoman, Frances Wright, to the United States in 1820; and it lasted some fifty years. During her stay, she was outspoken on theology, slavery, and the social degradation of women. For her, the issues of both Negro and woman's rights turned on the question of the innate worth of all persons, and the theological foundations for these movements were secure.

For two decades then, women became more educated and more enraged over the inhumanity of man to man and woman. So the meeting of Elizabeth Cady Stanton (1816-1902) and Lucretia Collins Mott (1793-1880) in 1840 was destined to be a wedding of complementary ideas that would be fully consummated with the passage of the fifteenth Amendment thirty years later. Mrs. Stanton, born and bred to the appreciation of legal process as the daughter of a judge and the wife of a lawyer, was a perfect partner for Mrs. Mott, herself a preacher and the wife of a Quaker minister. The meeting occurred in London, at the World's Anti-Slavery Convention, 1840, where Mrs. Mott, along with seven other women delegates to the conference was rejected and confined to the gallery. Both men and women were indignant over the incident and it riveted attention on the issue of women's rights. Eight years and several babies later, Elizabeth Stanton and Lucretia Mott met again at the Stanton home in Seneca Falls, New York, and drew up a Declaration of Sentiments, which was intentionally modeled on the Declaration of Independence.[9]

Included in the Declaration were twelve resolutions, all of which were adopted at the Seneca Falls Convention, July 19 and 20, 1848. Almost three hundred people attended and the signatures of sixty-eight women and thirty-two men were affixed to the Resolutions, the ninth of which read: "Resolved, That it is the duty of the women of this country to secure to themselves their sacred right to the elective franchise." [10] But there would be decades of retreats and postponement before this would be realized. This period ended with the split of the suffragist movement into the National Woman Suffrage Association (NWSA) under Mrs. Stanton and Susan B. Anthony and the more conservative American Woman Suffrage Association under the leadership of Lucy Stone. But it also ended with the abolitionists' success in the ratification of the Fourteenth and Fifteenth Amendments. The suffrage amendment omitted the word "sex"!

When the abolitionists forsook the suffragists, the women felt betrayed and Susan B. Anthony began the second major period by writing: "Man can no more feel, speak or act for woman than could the old slaveholder for his slave. The fact is, women are in chains, and their servitude is all the more debasing because they do not realize it." [11]

During this period, general distrust of the established parties, of unionization of labor, and greater cleavage between the upper and middle classes culminated in the diffusion of the more liberal NWSA. Finally, a merger of the two groups produced a larger, less militant group that primarily wanted the vote. This had never been the sole aim of the Big Three (Stanton, Mott, and Anthony); they wanted equal work and educational opportunities, as well as legal reforms concerning inheritance, divorce, property rights, and the guardianship of children.

Then followed the third period (1890-1920) fraught with many issues including social work, temperance, and labor laws; and many new feminists formed various and sundry new groups. However, for most suffragists, the struggle was single-issue dominated—getting the vote. One of the greatest blows to feminism, however, was the publication of Sigmund Freud's works on dream interpretation and sexuality. And the albatross, "Anatomy is destiny" was born to be woman's twentieth-century burden until Betty Friedan would shoot it down in 1963 and Germaine Greer would attempt to bury it in 1970.[12]

What happened to the public image of women as the new century was born? Since the ice was broken in the "thinking," masculine fields of medicine, law, the ministry, and business, would women flood these fields? Hardly! These were not ladylike professions; so women turned to fields more appropriate to "female character," the helping professions. They became lower-grade school teachers, social workers, nurses, and librarians. In a sense, these roles were viewed simply as extensions of their domestic roles; and because they were auxiliary positions, subordinate status and lower pay were justified.

Organized religion for the most part could not tolerate the continued agitation of women for public rights and recognition. For this reason, probably even more significant to the movement than the disastrous impact of the writings of Freud were the volumes produced by Elizabeth Stanton and a committee of twenty-three in 1895, *The Woman's Bible.* It not only acknowledged a male-dominated church, but also a Judeo-Christian heritage of female oppression.[13]

And so the Susan B. Anthony Amendment was passed June, 1919, and ratified by August 26, 1920, to be henceforth known as the Nineteenth Amendment. The period that followed was one of anti-climax and the larger movement for total women's rights simmered for forty years. Except for the National Woman's Party, there seemed not to be even a whispered "What now?"

The New Women's Movements

In retrospect, it seems altogether appropriate that the catalyst, not for a revived but a new women's rights movement, would be an author and her best-selling book. In 1963, Betty Friedan's *The Feminine Mystique* proclaimed to more than a million buyers that woman's state in the mid-twentieth century was "voluntary servitude." After achieving her highest educational level and her greatest public participation by 1950, the American woman, idol to the women of the world, settled down to a beatific complacency as the Johnnies came marching back from war, finished college, and reentered the business world. Only a decade of such apparent apathy was enough to produce the backlash of a new brand of women's organizations. Their chief distinction, according to Roberta Salper, is that, unlike their nineteenth-century counterparts, militant women in the 1970's who view their liberation as "revolutionary" are the norm rather than the exception.[14]

The passage of the Civil Rights Act, 1964, which included a ban on sex discrimination in employment opportunities under Title VII, was not enough. Women's groups began to proliferate and their acronyms were soon a match for those of the New Deal organizations of the 1930's. At least three patterns appear:

1. *Equality in Economic, Social, and Political Life.* These groups largely follow in the wake of Betty Friedan, discontented wives and professional women who prefer to "work solidly for reform within the 'establishment.' " Probably the largest, widest-known, and best-organized is National Organization for Women (NOW) founded in 1966. There are an estimated seven hundred chapters with members in all fifty states.[15] Other groups similar to NOW, in that they lobby for equal opportunity, pay, and advancement in the labor market, are:

Women's Equity Actions League (WEAL, 1968) splintered from NOW primarily over the question of abortion. It provides information about discrimination and work opportunities. A conservative pressure group, by 1974 it had initiated legal action in several hundred cases charging sex discrimination in areas of education, work, and taxation.

Human rights for Women (HRW, 1968) was established in Washington, D. C., and concerns itself primarily with free legal

aid to any woman involved in sex discrimination suits.
Federally Employed Women (FEW, 1968) works solely for
abolishing discrimination toward women in federal positions.
2. *Radical Feminists and Proponents of the New Left and Old
Left.*[16] These groups began in 1967 as a spin-off from NOW
in the formation of the *New York Radical Women* with the
slogan: "Sisterhood is powerful." This group introduced the
consciousness-raising rap sessions which are used by many
others in the radical camp. Many pulled out from the Civil
Rights movement of the 1960's, particularly from the Student
Non-Violent Coordinating Council (SNCC) and the Students
for a Democratic Society (SDS), due to the sexism practiced
by them. Many of these feminists are antiestablishment on a
universal scale. They are not only burning bras and demonstrating at beauty pageants; they are anti-family, anti-religion,
anti-femininity, and they call for a new socialism:

Women's International Terrorist Conspiracy from Hell
(WITCH, 1968) is loosely organized and suits its tactics to the
occasion. This grew out of the NYRW meeting in 1968.

Redstockings (1968), another division of NYRW, developed
the language and psychology of sisterhood. They became the
heart of radical feminism, under the leadership of Shulamith
Firestone and Ellen Willis, with the belief that personal and
social experience cannot be separated. Hence, they focused on
consciousness-raising techniques and became more militant
than their parent NYRW.

Society for Cutting Up Men (SCUM) is one of the most radical
groups, with members who are aggressive, strident, and intent
on overthrow of the major systems of society. Unfortunately,
their ideals for being domineering, vicious, spiteful, and egoistic
have often become the stereotype of feminists by those who
are their uninformed opponents.

3. *Women's Caucuses in Professional Organizations.* These
groups were rather spontaneous forces that formed in the Modern Language Association, American Political Science Association, American Historical Association, American Sociological

Association, and other disciplines. They were aimed primarily at achieving equal recognition, leadership, and status in their particular professions. Most of these have combined philosophical premises with positive action.

As stated then, the motivations and goals of feminist organizations are as numerous and varied as the oppressions which they claim have been perpetrated against women in history. Nevertheless, from where we stand in the mid-1970's, so close perhaps as not to have a clear view of the "forest," there seem to be some over-riding points of consensus in their manifestos.[17] Briefly stated, they are:

Educational. Schools will not teach sexism through role stereotyping in textbooks, faculty, nor administration. They will recruit students and faculty without sex discrimination, providing equal opportunity for advancement in terms of ability and interest. Governance of these institutions at all levels will be shared equally by the sexes.

Economic. Pay should be commensurate to the work and not determined by sex. Working conditions, fringe benefits, and opportunities for promotion should be shared equally. Protective work laws should apply to both sexes, but consideration should be given to the insurance needs of women during pregnancy and childbirth. Government and industry should provide day care centers for working parents.

Political. The number of women participating in government at all levels and from voting to leadership must be increased. The most effective way for women to change a discriminating society is to be involved in "making government."

Legislative. Work laws should apply to and protect both men and women. Social Security provisions must be revised for the single and widowed women. Marriage, divorce, inheritance, and child custody laws should not be biased toward either sex.

Religious. There must be positive interpretation of biblical and church teachings on women. Programs of women's studies would increase their awareness of the need to expand their roles in the church. All Christians must understand that God and the church are not based on gender.

Social-Pyschological. Both beliefs and practices regarding sex must change. There are few innate behaviors (chiefly those related to reproduction), traits, or virtues that are inherited. Consequently, there are few, if any, roles that should be arbitrarily assigned all women (or men.)

Whither Feminism?

Are we far enough down the road in realizing these goals of the women's liberation movement that we can foresee a time—in a decade, a generation, the year 2000—when such organizations will be obsolete, having eliminated the oppressions that precipitated the vigor and stamina of their being? Most feminists (and other females!) would probably give a resounding "NO!" What, then, has been accomplished in this decade of the "new feminism?" Some of these are mentioned in other chapters of this book, but here are some landmarks of our changing milieu:

1964—Passage of the Civil Rights Act, with the Title VII section providing equal work opportunities and banning sex discrimination.

1967—The United Nations Declaration on Women's Rights, November 11.

1968—The first black woman, Shirley Chisholm, a New York Democrat, elected to the United States House of Representatives. Her comment, "The cheerful old darky on the plantation and the happy little homemaker are equally stereotypes drawn by prejudice. . . . If I can win office how much more hope should that give to white women who have only one handicap?" [18]

1969—Women's Caucus in National Council of Churches affirms: "Nowhere is the situation of women better illustrated than in our male-dominated and male-oriented churches."

1970—New York state liberalizes its abortion law. San Diego State University offers the first women's studies program.

1971—Equal Employment Opportunities Commission

(EEOC) warns, "We will use every resource at our command to break the grip of Anglo males on virtually every good job in the [public utilities] industry." [19]

1972—The Equal Rights Amendment passes in the House of Representatives with 350:15 and in the Senate 84:8.

1973—The United States Supreme Court rules no state can deny a woman her right to choose childbirth or abortion.

—The EEOC orders several major corporations to pay reparations to women for discrimination in hiring and promotion.

—The first woman Armed Forces chaplain was commissioned into the Navy.

—The first graduate program in women's studies was established at Sarah Lawrence College through a grant of $140,000 from the Rockefeller Foundation.

1974—Ada Evans becomes the first black woman mayor in the United States at Fairplay, Colorado.

—The proclamation setting August 26 as Woman's Equality Day is one of President Ford's first official acts.

The Christian woman and her church cannot ignore nor halt the women's liberation frontal attack. Indeed, as the whole thesis of this chapter suggests, the movement is entering, though belatedly, the church of God who is above gender. What will hopefully evolve, both in the sacred and secular spheres of our experience, is a society of persons, where opportunity, advancement, privilege, and relationships are not predestined by sex chromosomes. This will not be achieved by unsexual patterns of utter conformity nor by mere swapping of sex role traits. We have yet to define fully what a society is like when based on "humanness," which appreciates male-female differences along with distinctions in gifts, intelligence, and interests without attaching rank-values to them.

Theologian Harvey Cox has established the Christian motif for this period in the history of persons. It is his preamble to "Eight Theses on Female Liberation:"

God's cosmic purpose is the liberation and maturation of all human beings, and indeed, of all creation, to full participation in an ecstatic universe of love and joy. The current movements of liberation—of colonialized people, Blacks, peasants, women, and even of nature from its thralldom to man's greed—are the groanings and reaching-outs of this universal process. As such, people of faith rightly sing about these stirrings, struggle with them, and discern in their anger and aspiration the sure signals of a coming new era.[20]

Notes

1. Cf. Mary McDermott, Shideler, "Male and Female Created He Them," and Robert S. Brightman, "The Other Half of God," *Religion in Life,* XLIII (Spring, 1974), pp. 60-67, 68-78.

2. L. T. Hobhouse, *Morals in Evolution* (New York: Rinehart and Winston, 1921), p. 159.

3. For a fuller discussion of women in earlier civilizations, see Harkness, *Women in Church and Society.*

4. An excellent treatment of women in these centuries is found in Eugene A. Hecker, *A Short History of Women's Rights,* 2nd ed. revised (Conn.: Greenwood Press, 1914, 1917), chap. 6.

5. William Robert Carr, Introduction to John Stuart Mill, *The Subjection of Women* (M.I.T. Press, 1970 edition of 1869 original).

6. Charles F. Adams, ed., *Familiar Letters of John and Abigail Adams* (Boston: Houghton-Mifflin, 1898). This quotation is given in Eleanor Flexner, *Century of Struggle* (Cambridge: Belknap Press, 1959), p. 15.

7. Cf. Harkness, *op. cit.,* pp. 101-111.

8. Phebe A. Hanaford, Daughters of America or Women of the Century (Augusta, Mo.: True and Co., 1882) cited in Harkness, *op. cit.,* pp. 231-323.

9. Cited entirely by William O'Neill, *The Woman Movement* (New York: Barnes & Noble, 1969), pp. 108-111.

10. *Ibid.*

11. Quoted by Nan Trent, "Prime Movers for Feminists," (Christian Science Monitor News Service), *The Shreveport Times* (La.), Wednesday, April 25, 1973, Section B, p. 1.

12. Betty Friedan, *The Feminine Mystique* (New York: W. W. Norton, 1963) and Germaine Greer, *The Female Eunuch* (New York: Bantam Books, 1970).

13. Harkness, *op. cit.,* pp. 140-141.

14. Robert Salper, *Female Liberation, History and Current Politics* (New York: Knopf, 1972), p. 13.

15. Judith Hole and Ellen Levine, *Rebirth of Feminism* (New York: Quadrangle Books, 1971), p. 95.

16. The "text" of this group is Ann Koedt, Ellen Levin, Anita Rapone, *Radical Feminism* (New York: Quadrangle Books, 1973).

17. An excellent comprehensive treatment of the motivations and goals of the WLM may be found in Letsinger, *op. cit.,* pp. 25-77.

18. Quoted by Nan Trent, *op. cit.*

19. *Ibid.*

20. Harvey Cox, "Eight Theses on Female Liberation," *Christianity and Crisis* 31 (October 4, 1971): p. 199.

6
Myths About Men and Women
Harry N. Hollis, Jr.

When a well-educated young woman was presented to King James I and her knowledge of Latin, Greek, and Hebrew praised, James asked: "But can she spin?"

I married for ambition. Carlyle has exceeded all that my wildest hopes ever imagined for him, and I am miserable.—Mrs. Thomas Carlyle

A discussion of myths about men and women cannot be neatly arranged in a system, because there is nothing organized about these myths in our society. They are haphazard and random. They are rooted deep in our soil. They are stubbornly mouthed from parent to child, from generation to generation. These myths are ridiculed, attacked, and dissected. But they still survive.

It is going to be extremely difficult, therefore, for society to outgrow childish mythologies about men and women. But, in Christianity we have the resources to do so. It is the thrust of this book that Christianity offers us hope to face problems related to the freedom of all human beings in our society.

We will discuss here several of the more persistent myths which keep deflecting people from truth about men and women. Furthermore, we will evaluate these myths from a Christian perspective. No doubt there are other myths that need to be examined. No doubt some of the myths discussed here overlap each other. The most important goal of this chapter, however, is to begin to recognize the presence and the tenaciousness of these myths in our lives. Here are a dozen myths which hamper human liberation.

The Sugar-and-Spice Myth

This first myth concerns the nature of being female, and it is summed up in this children's poem:

What are little girls made of?
Sugar and spice and everything nice;
That's what little girls are made of.

Of course, this is an innocent children's rhyme, but it has sinister implications for an understanding of the nature of a female. What it means is that little girls are expected to sweeten things up for us. They are not competitive or rough or aggressive, but sweet! Little girls are made of spice. They add some zest, some flavor, even a little temptation to life! And little girls are characterized by everything that is nice. They do not misbehave; they are proper. They keep morals for us.

Now, what is wrong with this description? As far as it goes, nothing! The rhyme is okay, but the myth is not! Sugar and spice and everything nice are fine ingredients, but they are not enough to make a full human being. What happens, therefore, is that this myth leads to placing women on a pedestal. Up there, in their seclusion, they are protected from reality. Up there they can serve as keepers of morality. Of course, the men will misbehave with the not-so-nice girls down below, but the mythology will remain intact. The "sugar-and-spice" myth keeps women in their place, being seen and not heard, at least not heard on important matters.

From a Christian point of view, therefore, this "sugar-and-spice" myth is to be rejected. The Bible teaches that women are full human beings. They are not just showpieces to be encased under glass. They are freed by Christ, not from life but for life. All human beings are to be salt and light penetrating the world. None of us, woman or man, is to escape to a pedestal somewhere to avoid the realities of life. Women are called not to escape in order to enjoy dainty dresses and demitasses of tea, but to be companions in a real world where people laugh and cry, where people are clean and dirty, where things are nice and sometimes not so nice.

The "sugar-and-spice" myth is a negation of a Christian understanding of the nature of woman. It does contain subtle truths, but it is incomplete. It refuses to allow women to be the humans God intended them to be. Nursery rhymes are fine, unless they are taken seriously by adults, and, for that matter, by children. Then they become very dangerous. The "sugar-and-spice" myth often distorts the child's understanding of what it means to be a girl or a woman. It gives them a subhuman model of personhood. The "sugar-and-spice" myth must be rejected.

The Puppy-Dog-Tail Myth

Society also mythologizes about what it means to be a male. The rest of the children's rhyme, according to the version I learned, goes like this:

> What are little boys made of?
> Snails and nails, and puppy-dogs' tails;
> That's what little boys are made of.

It is a mistake, of course, to read too much into the words of this rhyme, but, nevertheless, there are some interesting parallels between the words and the traits expected of little boys. Snails get dirty; so do little boys. They are expected to. Nails are tough; so are little boys. There is not anything much more active than a puppy-dog's tail except perhaps a little boy (or a little girl). Little boys are expected to be active and aggressive.

This myth about the nature of the male is as pervasive as the "sugar-and-spice" myth. It teaches that little boys are to be tough and aggressive. They are contrasted with the little girls, who are sweet and nice. Boys will take care of the action and girls will handle the morals. This myth leads to the view that tenderness and masculinity are antithetical. Indeed, it leads right to the pages of many adventure magazines where exaggerated masculinity is preached and some writers practice regular hostility toward women.

Christianity stands in judgment of this "puppy-dog-tail" myth because Christians are called to be the full human beings God intended. Hostility between the sexes is eradicated in Jesus Christ, in whom there is neither male nor female. Fellowship is made possible. These myths, on the contrary, lead to hostility. They teach that the male and female are absurdly different from each other.

Unisex, which is probably more popular in the media than it is in reality, must be rejected by Christians. At the same time, we must also reject the hyper-gender preoccupation of the "puppy-dog-tail" and "sugar-and-spice" myths. As we seek to understand human nature, it is good to remember that it is *human* nature: we are humans, who happen to be created males and females. Differences which are a part of our nature cannot be ignored. At the same time, the common humanity and the full personhood of males and females must be acknowledged and celebrated.

The Debased-Sexual-Object Myth

Here is a myth based on a theory of Sigmund Freud which is summarized in his statement: "Where they [civilized men] love they do not desire and where they desire they cannot love." [1] This myth is often whispered, but it is all too prevalent in our society. Indeed, in some cultures, this myth is carried so far that a man relates to one woman as his wife and mother of his children and to another as his mistress with whom he has sexual fulfillment. Freud contended that a man feels his respect for a woman as a restriction upon his sexual activity and full potency.[2] Many who have never heard of Freud have, nevertheless, practiced what he predicted by turning to women in lower economic classes in the hope of finding uninhibited sexual pleasure.

This particularly tenacious, yet crippling, myth leads to the creation of two classes of women in society. It results in an entrenched double standard. The "nice" girls, who are put on a pedestal, are expected to bear children and raise a family, and the "wicked" women are kept down below for use as sexual objects.

Does Christianity have anything to say about this myth? It certainly does. The "debased-sexual-object" myth is contrary to biblical teaching about women and about sex. It ignores the union between sexual intercourse and the marriage covenant which the Bible teaches. It misses the celebration of sex. It fails to take into account the fact that many men do have desire for women they respect and to whom they are married.

Christianity stands firmly against the creation of two classes of women: the good and the bad. It teaches instead that all women have dignity and worth. It has special condemnation for those who take advantage of the poor, who are economically vulnerable and thus sometimes easily manipulated into exploitive sexual affairs.

The debased sexual object myth was wrong when Freud offered it as an explanation of reality, and it is still wrong. To be sure, Freud was describing what he had seen in some of his patients, but he jumped from such limited data to a particularly unhealthy generalization. The "debased-sexual-object" myth should be rejected by Christian men and women.

The Happy-Housewife Myth

The foundation for this belief is the oft-repeated "a woman's place in the home." What this means is that women are made to be mothers and housekeepers; these are their sole responsibilities.

Now, it follows from this myth that if woman's place is in the home, she does not need skills acquired by people who work outside the home. She does not need to understand much about the outside affairs of life. She should not aggressively pursue outside interests, of course. She needs to know a lot about Dr. Spock and Pampers and Pablum. But such matters as career fulfillment, international peace, and political representation should not interest her.

The people who say that a woman's place is in the home really do not know much about contemporary women at all. The modern mother and wife is already out of the home a great deal, chauffeuring children, negotiating to get a portable TV repaired, picking up groceries, straightening out a charge account foul-up, going to the PTA bake sale, singing in the adult choir. The issue is really not whether women are in or outside the home. They have long ago broken through the home barricades in their station wagons. The question is whether or not women will be outside the home in useful or in frivolous activity.

The Christian message speaks to the "happy-housewife" myth. Christianity calls on us to recognize the deeper hurts of people. The truth is that many women suffer deeply because they feel unfulfilled in our myth-oriented society. Our response should not be to imprison women behind four walls but to help them find fulfillment at home and wherever Christ's calling leads them.

Christianity affirms motherhood, to be sure, but an exclusive focus on motherhood to the detriment of all other aspects of a woman's character is a mistake. It can leave the mother with a desperate void when the children depart the home. And an exclusive focus on motherhood will also contribute to the population explosion which is already bringing famine, hunger, and disease in many parts of the world. Christianity teaches that parenthood is a blessing, but it rejects the obligation to reproduce indiscriminately.

The "happy-housewife" myth fails to understand the nature of some biblical teachings. It fails to distinguish between the changeless gospel and the need to apply the gospel to changing society. It fails to distinguish between the culture of Bible times and the gospel itself. The roles of women dare not be based on the patriarchal, rural society of the past. In the urban world, something else is required. Many women may choose to focus on the role of housewife, but this should be by choice not coercion. The "happy-housewife" myth must give way to acceptance of women as full human beings with varied interests and roles in a changing world.

The Freudian-Predestination Myth

Sigmund Freud is at least partially responsible for this myth which centers on the view that "anatomy is destiny." Because we have been given a certain anatomy, we are therefore predestined to a certain kind of behavior. Now, anatomy does make a difference, but not the difference Freud predicted. He said that little girls begin to believe that they have a "genital deficiency" because their anatomy is different from the male. This has a profound impact on their lives and leads to behavior over which they have very little control. Their destiny, then, is dictated by their anatomy. Their envy of male anatomy leads to passivity, dependence, sexual frigidity, and general incompetence.[3]

Of course, if anatomy predetermines the destiny of females, it does the same for males. Freudian predestination leads to a belief that the male is superior. Thus, the predestination myth dictates sexual inequality. It assures the fact that there will be an absence of the sexual exchange of two equals who share the totality of life.

From a Christian point of view, this myth must be soundly rejected. The destiny of every human being is determined not by anatomy, but by the relationship that the man and woman have to God in Jesus Christ. This is not to say that the biological differences in men and women should be ignored; nor is it to say that given the reality of these differences, there will not be different experiences and thus different kinds of behavior. But Freud was too limited in his exposure to healthy women. He wrongly assumed that all women were like his wife, select group of friends, and patients.

Any predestination, including Freudian predestination, stands contrary to the freedom of an individual in Jesus Christ. The "anatomy is destiny" myth has brainwashed women and men about their true nature as human beings. Such a myth deserves strong Christian opposition.

The Boys'-Night-Out-Myth

Here is a myth which is expressed by anthropologist Lionel Tiger when he says, "Every man needs a night out with the boys." [4] According to this myth, which Tiger tries to clothe in scientific respectability, men seek out the companionship of other men because it is a biological necessity to do so. This "boys'-night-out" myth, as articulated by Tiger and others, stresses an exaggerated masculinity and calls for the segregation of sexes in education, recreation, politics, and the professions. [5] The argument goes that men who are too actively dominated by their wives and families "may lose a certain constructive maleness of consequence to many of their activities." [6] Although wives may fear their husbands' leaving the home to associate with all-male groups, this fear is foundless because the males do not collectively seek out other women; instead, they drink, talk, or gamble, according to Tiger. [7]

Now, it is certainly true that some masculine activities outside the home are healthy and normal. But to give this kind of activity the legitimacy of scientific and biological justification is dangerous. Drinking, talking (translate that gossiping), and gambling are hardly worthy activities. Nor are many other activities that take place in an all-male socializing.

What does the Christian message say to the "boys'-night-out" myth? Christianity affirms *koinonia* between human beings. It recognizes the need for fellowship and companionship between people of the same and different sexes. But it also rejects the mischief-making that often occurs in all-male (and for that matter all-female) gatherings. The boys' night out ethic is potentially dangerous to the family. What is called for is not the diminution of the family but the expansion of family ties to include many friends. We are not called to escape family life but to live in our families in such a way that our horizons are broadened.

In spite of Tiger's protest to the contrary, inherent in the "boys'-night-out" myth is the view that a man escapes the family for sexual experimentation and diversity. It is not a far step from "the boys' night out" to "boys will be boys" to "boys will sow their wild oats." Christianity stands against these ideas as well. It calls for fidelity to family and friends, and it rejects any kind of reversion to juvenile behavior where there is no adult responsibility for immorality.

The He's-Got-the-Brain Myth

This myth is founded on the idea that man is rational, while woman is emotional. It was well expressed by Lord Chesterfield: "Women, then, are only children of the larger growth. . . . For solid reasoning and good sense I never knew in my life one that had it." Few contemporary people would put the matter so boldly, but many men, and, for that matter, women, believe the "he's-got-the-brain" myth. They would say: Look at the artists of our culture. Look at the writers, the presidents, the military leaders, the chairmen of the boards, look at the inventors, the movers and doers, the thinkers. Overwhelmingly all these people have been men.

Glenda Nochlin asks the question in another way: "Why are there no great women artists?" [8] The answer is not that women are incapable of such greatness; rather the solution to this query is found in the institutions of our society. Systematically, women have been denied education and opportunities and experiences in our society which would equip them to be artists. Nochlin argues that "it was made institutionally impossible for women to achieve artistic excellence or success on the same footing as men, no matter what the potency of their so-called talent or genius, or their lack of this mysterious ingredient." [9]

Christianity rejects this myth which sees woman essentially as an emotional, silly, brainless plaything. It opposes the idea that man was given the brains at creation and that little was left for woman. Christianity stands in judgment on situations which keep any person from the just education and experience which he deserves.

As Christians, we are called not to translate faith into a private ethic with no social responsibility. Instead we are called to penetrate the structures of society and use Christ's truth to remove any injustices that exist. This means opposing the institutionalization of the "he's-got-the-brain" myth.

The Asensuous Woman Myth

The idea that women see sex as a regrettable necessity is the foundation for this myth. To be sure, it overlaps some earlier myths already mentioned, but it is persistent and dangerous enough to be discussed separately. In the past, it was believed by man that women did not have any sexual desire. A woman was an attractive incubator for babies. She was not expected to feel any sexual pleasure and her sexual needs were usually not considered, because, according to some, they did not exist. Any woman who acted differently was considered to be immoral or at least abnormal.

The remnants of sexual negativism in our culture feed this myth. In spite of the sensational literature about sensuous women, many men and some women still believe that sex is a regrettable necessity for most women. Where does this myth lead? Obviously, it can result in unfulfilled men and women. It means that many couples miss out on the excitement and exhilaration that comes in celebrating the joy of sex in a covenant of total giving.

Christianity stands clearly against this myth, because it teaches that God created man and woman to be one flesh. Sex is to be celebrated and enjoyed as long as it is used in the responsible way in which God intended it to be used. Both women and men are created with the capacity for sexual celebration and fulfillment.

The "asensuous-woman" myth views sex as a necessary evil and places sex in the Fall instead of in creation. It is a misreading of Scripture and a misreading of God's intention. Christians should oppose this crippling and discriminatory myth.

The Matriarchy Myth

A good deal of attention is given these days to the view that the American woman really mothers and thus controls the man. Philip Wylie has crusaded against such "momism." Eve Meriam talks about the growing preoccupation with this myth in American culture: "Farewell to the little woman puttering in her petunia garden. In her stead strides the All-American Female: she doesn't raise flowers, she eats them. Ordering our tastes, conditioning our entire culture, with money and mores in her grip, she indoctrinates us all from prenatal to unhappy ever after. We may free ourselves from the dictatorship of Big Brother, but not from Sister Sue." [10]

The myth implies that man is being demasculinized by an over-aggressive woman. He is imprisoned and stifled by a matriarchal potentate. His being is threatened and he must fight back.

Christianity stands in judgment of the "matriarchy" myth, because it is simply not true. No doubt, some families have dominating mothers. No doubt, women have gained power in some areas of society. No doubt, many women do seek to exert undue authority over the men in their lives. But Christianity demands truth, and the truth is that many women are forced into these roles because of the absence of male responsibility.

There can be little doubt, furthermore, that men control the institutions in our society which exercise power. Of course, Christianity stands against the attempt of men or women to dominate other human beings in a manipulative fashion. It stands against what Eve Meriam calls "Big Mommies and little daddies." [11] It opposes replacing a patriarchy with a matriarchy. But the truth is that matriarchy is not an immediate threat. Women are not trying to take over society. They are trying to secure basic rights and human dignity. As Christians, we are called to help them.

The Man-Behind-the-Desk Myth

Parallel to the "happy-housewife" myth is the view that a man's place is at the office or the factory or on the road. This is based on some truth, to be sure, because men are responsible for meeting the needs of their families, just as women are. But this myth rigidifies roles. It says that man must earn the money while woman tends the house.

It thus lets the man off the hook from any responsibility in the home which might be conceived as "woman's work." Today most housework is more physical than office work. Pushing a sweeper is more physical than pushing a pencil! But many supposedly physical men ignore this.

What has been said before concerning the difference between the changeless Christian gospel and the changing culture to which the gospel must be applied can now be reiterated. Differences between men and women may not change, but ways that these differences are expressed in roles, in vocations, and in responsibilities may change. The pursuit of a career by a man is expected; the neglect of any responsibility by the male in the home must be rejected. Christianity calls for a family relationship where there is mutual sharing in all areas of responsibility. The "man-behind-the-desk" myth must be corrected.

The Man-Is-the-Enemy Myth

Here is a view that all men are chauvinists. Thus, all men are looked upon by some militant feminists as *the* enemy. A Boston militant renamed herself Betsy Warrior and wrote in a woman's liberation newspaper: "Sooner or later, if we are effective, men will become hostile. We have to be prepared to accept this fact. Not only accept it but segregate ourselves from man in many situations, to allow ourselves freedom from their criticisms, opinions and dominance. . . . As long as we are entangled in personal relationships in group situations with men, we won't be able to clearly analyze our positions and will have a vested interest in not making males too hostile."

Most myths contain a kernel of truth and this one is no exception. There is much too much chauvinism in our society. But this does not call for the cynical attitude that all men are the enemies of women. Such an attitude only insures continued hostility between the sexes. The "man-is-the-enemy" myth ignores the many men who treat women not as demons or deities but as human beings.

A Christian understanding of sinfulness speaks to this myth. We learn through Scripture that sin has entered the lives of all of us. This means that men do sin against women through exploitation and manipulation. But men have no monopoly on sin. Everyone—men and women—are sinful. But in Jesus Christ the barriers between people can be broken down. In Christ there is neither male nor female. And Christianity stands firmly against any myth to the contrary.

The Maladjusted-Feminist Myth

All women's liberation supporters are really frustrated women who are interested in participating in such nonsense as bra burning. At least, this is a myth which is quite persistent in our society. The problem with this myth is that it fails to take into account those women who do not fit this stereotype.

To be sure there are some women who are maladjusted liberationists. They enter this movement to make mischief. They do the cause of genuine liberation great harm. But there are many more decent, gifted, sensitive women who are working quietly or visibly to bring about change. This myth ignores these women and thus ignores reality.

Christianity calls men, and for that matter women, to be sensitive to the plight of women in our society. Given the reality of institutional discrimination and individual exploitation, men should be involved in assisting women to achieve their rights. To belittle decent women, who are resisting discrimination, is to ignore Christ's call to set at liberty the captives.

Conclusion

We have examined a dozen myths about men and women. There are many other myths that deserve our scrutiny and opposition. Recently, I asked participants in a conference to suggest some myths about men and women and here are some of their responses: the "all-men-are-alike" myth (this refers to the view that males are only interested in women as sex partners); the "happily-ever-after" myth ("They were married and lived happily ever after."); the "happy-breadwinner" myth (all men really enjoy going out to earn a living); the myth of the "bored-housewife;" the "behind-every-successful-man-is-a-good-woman" myth; the "marriage-is-the-only-thing-in-life" myth.

The myths we have analyzed, plus these only mentioned here, point to the serious confusion and misinformation about females and males in our society. It is the purpose of this book to oppose these myths. Christians have the opportunity and the responsibility to explode these myths so that we can all be more fully human.

Notes

1. Sigmund Freud, "On the Universal Tendency to Debasement in the Sphere of Love," *The Standard Edition of the Complete Psychological Works of Sigmund Freud,* James Strachey, trans. (London: The Hogarth Press, 1910), XI, 183.
2. *Ibid.,* p. 185.
3. Betty Roszak and Theodore Roszak, eds., *Masculine/Feminine* (New York: Harper & Row, 1969), p. 20.
4. See Lionel Tiger, "Why Men Need a Boys' Night Out," Roszak and Roszak, *op. cit.,* p. 38.
5. *Ibid.,* p. 39.
6. *Ibid.,* p. 46.
7. *Ibid.,* p. 45.
8. Glenda Nochlin, "Why There Are No Great Women Artists," *Woman in Sexist Society,* edited by Vivian Gornick and Barbara K. Moran (New York: Basic Books, Inc., 1971), pp. 344-366.
9. *Ibid.,* p. 365.
10. Eve Meriam, *After Noah Slammed the Door* (New York: World Publishing Company, 1964), p. 103.
11. *Ibid.,* p. 121.

7

A Christian Critique of Institutional Discriminations Against Women

Sarah Frances Anders

Hardly a day passed in the life and ministry of Jesus that he did not confront issues growing out of the institutional discriminations of his culture. He reacted revolutionarily toward persons that society had placed in unvarying categories of low estate—Samaritans, lepers, women, criminals, the mentally ill, and capitulators to Roman authority, to name only a few. He met resistance, to the point of death, from institutional leaders who felt threatened by his life-style and teachings, particularly those in organized religion and government.

Those concerned with the liberation of humans, from every manner of discrimination, worry about a society that still seems to be predicated on Gunnar Myrdal's stated paradox of spoken equality and practiced inequality. Social scientists, as well as the feminist organizations, have suggested that women in America have belonged to a caste system as surely as Indians, blacks, Orientals, or Chicanos. To grant such a premise is not to say that all women have stayed in place; indeed a surprising number have become "over-casts" as compared with outcasts! Nor does this suggest that all males are chauvinistic and threatened by a human liberation movement. Especially the Christian of either sex should recognize that sex roles are a different phenomenon from gender and that often social expectations for masculine and feminine are harmful to both sexes.

Bastions of the Status Quo

As in Jesus' day, some institutions are more resistant than others to changing tradition, whether that tradition is based on truth or not. In other chapters, we deal with two of these institutions—the family and the organized church. It is appropriate to look now at two other protectors of "things as they have been."

Business and the Professions

In 1970, James D. Hodgson, Secretary of Labor, was quoted, "Sex bias in the labor market is more subtle and pervasive than against any other minority group." [1] No area of American life, certainly, is more shackled by mythology about women than the workaday world. A sampling of such myths would include:

"This field is not for women."

"Women don't want full-time careers; they want temporary work for pin money for themselves or extras for the family."

"You can expect more absenteeism and turnover if you hire women."

"Why do they want to work—they already control most of the wealth in the country."

"Girls are better at details and just aren't brought up to take the rough competition of the work-world."

"Their emotional unpredictability would make them unsuited for the pressures of high-level decision making in this position."

In spite of history's attestation to women as co-laborers with men throughout the gathering, herding, and agricultural periods, the industrial revolution has produced the image of women as a reserve labor force, standing ready to "yo-yo" in and out of the economy as men were needed to defend the country or new lower-level jobs appeared. The expectation that this image will be changed is based on the fact that there has been steady increase in the proportion of women who work outside the home (now almost half) and in their representation in the labor force (almost 40 percent). If a woman remains single (and 10 percent will), she will average forty-five working years, longer than the average male. As a married woman, she will still work an average of thirty-five years, only eight years less than a man. [2]

Women make up a formidable thirty-three million working force. They hardly work for fun or frills when 60 percent of them are single, widowed, divorced, or married to a man making less than $7,000 a year.[3] Almost six million of them are heads of households and the number is increasing at the rate of a hundred thousand annually.[4] Nevertheless, although their economic needs and satisfaction may be as great as men's, the salary gap between male and female workers is increasing and other discriminations are obvious. Women's salaries average only 59 percent those of men, the greatest disparity occurring in the professional and managerial groups, where the differential is as much as $5,000. This is the situation more than a decade after the Equal Pay Act of 1963. Does it strike you as incongruous in a nation in which 65 percent of the adults are church-affiliates and the vast majority of these "Christian" by faith, that claims made against individual companies could amount to over one-half million dollars in wage discrimination? One 1974 case involving Corning Glass Works totaled $600,000 in wage adjustment for women night workers.

About the same time, American Telephone and Telegraph Company paid $45.7 million to nonmanagement employees, after having paid, only the year before, $30 million to management personnel who were victims of discrimination—most of them women.[5]

Almost 80 percent of the women workers are found in lower white-collar and domestic/service occupations. Less than 15 percent of these were unionized by the late 1960's and able to bargain for better conditions; so, it is not surprising that their incomes were generally under $5,000.[6] What is surprising is that the Chase National Bank estimated that the United States housewife held the equivalent of a 99.6-hour job paying $13,391.56![7]

Shirley Chisholm, in a speech in the House of Representatives soon after her election, pointed out that women constituted only about 2 percent of the bona fide managerial class of workers, that there were no women on the AFL-CIO Council, nor on the Supreme Court! [8] *Fortune* surveyed the thousand largest industrial companies and the three hundred largest nonindustrial companies for the top three executives and any directors earning more than $30,000 in 1971-72. Of some sixty-five hundred officers and directors in this earning category, only eleven were women! They also discovered that nine of these women in top management were helped along by family connections, by marriage, or by the fact that they helped organize the companies they preside over. [9]

The situation report in the professions is not encouraging either, for women make up:

- 7.6 percent of the 345,000 doctors
- 10.0 percent of the 350,000 plus scientists
- 2.8 percent of the 325,000 lawyers
- 20.0 percent of some 300,000 college professors and administrators
- 2.0 percent of 10,000 judges [10]

Women will make up more than one half of the 15.5 million growth in the labor force expected by 1979. [11] Prompted either by Christian attitude or the feminist movement, things are beginning to look more hopeful for them. Part of the direct impetus for change were (1) the Title VII section of the Civil Rights Act of 1964 with the subsequent Equal Employment Opportunities Commission (EEOC) and (2) the Executive Order 11246 (1972) which stated that all companies bidding for new or renewed federal contracts must file affirmative action programs for women. As one General Electric directive to all managers stated, concerning the women's movement: "This movement is not a fad or an aberration, but a major social force with great and growing impact on business and other social, political, and economic institutions. As such, it must be taken seriously by business managers." [12] And from George R. Vila, President of Uniroyal, Inc.: "Any company that overlooks women will be making a fatal mistake." [13]

Politics and Government

The women's movement into the political arena has been slow, but there are indications that the winds are shifting. Only last year a writer in *Ms.* magazine stated, "For women there is one acceptable entry route for Congress: come in as a Congressman's widow." [14] It was estimated in 1974 that 3,000 women would seek city, state, or national office during the year, three times the number who ran two years earlier. Among these would be 108 running for Congress, almost 700 for state legislatures, about 12 for lieutenant governor and 10 for governor. [15]

Many tactics have been used by chauvinists to keep a low profile on women in government positions. Three are worth identifying here: temperament, status, and role. First of all, women candidates may be seen as "too masculine" as Bella Abzug was in her New York Democratic race for Congress, or "too pretty and feminine" as others have been labeled. Often, their serious political comments are lost in the trivia of the reporting on their clothes, size, or voice. Secondly, women suffer in status if they are not taken seriously in their political pursuits as when CBS put down Sissy Farenthold by replacing the vice-presidential nomination speech for her with commercials. Lastly, women's roles in party organization may be confined to volunteer work in mail outs or coffee hours, and she may be given tribute by the phrase, "behind every good man. . . ." Should she dare run for office, she can be a veritable Amazon of talents and credentials, but the press may label her as a "housewife and mother of three." [16]

After two years of corruption and exposure in American politics, it may be the time for the "outs" to move in. In an Eagleton Institute Survey recently, 63 percent of the voters polled said that they would vote for a woman president! [17] On the national level in 1975, there are no women senators and eighteen representatives. The Nixon administration did not favor women with high level appointments, placing them primarily in executive secretarial positions or as consultants in consumer affairs. There are no cabinet nor justice women although there are five women ambassadors, one appointed by President Ford. Shirley M. Hufstedler is the only woman judge serving a higher court, the Ninth Court of Appeals. Kennedy established the President's Commission on the Status of Women on December 14, 1961, and had its report by November 11, 1963. President Johnson appointed at least one hundred women to top government positions and promoted two thousand or more to positions earning $10,000 and higher. He said at the time, "My whole aim in promoting women and picking out more women to serve in this administration is to underline our profound belief that we can waste no talent, we can frustrate no creative power, we can neglect no skill in our search for an open and just and challenging society." [18]

Women have been in low estate in federal civil service positions, with 77 percent of them in GS-1 to GS-6 ratings. The starting salary for GS-6 was $8,977 in 1974. Only 10 percent of the women are in GS-14 and GS-15 positions, but 43 percent of the men have these ratings.[19]

On the state level, in November, 1974, Ella Grasso of Connecticut became the first woman governor who did not succeed her husband in office. In that same nation-wide election, a woman was elected Lieutenant Governor of New York and another in North Carolina became the first chief justice of a state supreme court. Only 6 percent of the state legislators are women, and there are no women among the state attorney generals. However, women are good for state government, one recent paper at the American Political Science Association indicated. A study of 103 state women legislators showed them to be more intelligent, assertive, venturesome, imaginative and liberal in their attitudes than most women! [20] At the grass roots level, there are only about 30 women among the 18,500 mayors of United States towns and cities.[21] Recently, the woman elected mayor of San Jose, California, became the first woman to serve in a city of more than 500,000.

Modus Operandi for Change

Three institutionalized patterns of American behavior hold the most promise for change of attitudes and stereotypes regarding any minority: group legislation; education; and mass media. Laws can be quick to change, but resistance can create backlash movements as civil rights legislation did in the 1950's. Education is a more basic and desirable vehicle for behavior modification, but it often takes more than a generation to accomplish any significant change since there must be time to educate a new faculty and school board system, as well as to change images in textbooks. The communication media has the potential for being powerful and avant garde in shaping fads and fashions in behavior; but often it is more reflective than creative when it treats significant issues.

Law and the Legal Process [22]

Two nineteenth-century legislative acts laid the foundation for overthrowing many of "Jim Crow" laws operating against women: the 1867 law establishing a United States Office of Education which promptly concerned itself with upgrading female education; and the 1870 law providing equal pay for women in federal service. The latter was grossly misinterpreted and misused for almost ninety years to the disadvantage of women until Eleanor Roosevelt pressured for its reinterpretation in 1962.

Women's Equity Action League (WEAL) has used two pieces of legal action as a basis for hundreds of legal suits on grounds of sex discrimination, the Equal Pay Act of 1963 and the close-following Executive Order 11126. The former prohibits any discrimination in wages based on sex, and the EO 11126 provided for a Citizen's Advisory Council that would regularly report to the President on matters related to the treatment of women. Equally significant was EO 11246 (1965), already mentioned, which bird-dogged companies and schools that wanted federal contracts. WEAL initiated over three hundred law suits on behalf of women, primarily against law and medical schools. One case in point recently was Rutgers University which paid $395,000 to women and minority group faculty members not earning what white males were.[23]

A major development was the birth of the National Women's Political Caucus in 1970, a multi-partisan group aimed at "awakening, organizing, and asserting the vast political power represented by women." A number of successful legislative coups already were accomplished by 1972 when Congress finally completed favorable action on the Equal Rights Amendment, which said succinctly, "Equality of rights under the law shall not be denied or abridged by the United States or by any State on account of sex." At this writing, the ERA is still short of the necessary thirty-eight for ratification.

The Christian employer or employee dislikes resorting to legal action in order to obtain equitable treatment. Churches, conventions, and denominational colleges will do well to take note of the increasing possibility for such legal action in terms not only of minimum but equal wages for women in their employ. They may also have to show cause why church staffs, denominational personnel, faculties, and administration have not actively recruited and employed women.

Education

Sexism in education begins as early as formal training does, whether that be in preschool experiences or elementary school. It begins in the minds of mothers and early elementary teachers, as well as Sunday School teachers, who think of little girls in terms of adjectives such as cooperative, passive, sweet, sensitive, and obliging but think of little boys as being aggressive, mischievous, energetic, and adventuresome. Soon self-fulfilling prophecies are well on their way to becoming realities, as much so in the sexes as when an oppressed racial group begins to adopt the behaviors attributed to them through adjectives such as lazy, devious, untruthful, or thieving. Further support is given sexual stereotyping by lower-level readers, in which Bob plays

Little League ball, rough-houses, and plays with chemistry sets while Debbie plays house, tends her dolls, and gives tea parties. "Sex-aration" and "sex-ordination" are firmly entrenched in young minds by seven or eight years of age, because they understand that bosses are men and secretaries are women, doctors are men and nurses are women, ministers are men and nursery directors are women, second-grade teachers are women but their "bosses" are male principals. Early public education is female-predominant and male-dominant, for 85 percent of the teachers are women and only 21 percent of the principals [24] are women. By high school, female teachers are associated with literature, art, music, home economics; and men are in science, mathematics, woodwork/crafts or coaching, and the principal's office (97 percent).[25] Students may be alert enough to the power structure of the community by this time to observe the further dominance of men on school boards (90 percent) [26] and as superintendents of schools (99 percent).[27] Moreover, only two state superintendents of education are women.

Many studies document the loss of academic potential and self-esteem by girls during the educational process. More of them will complete high school, but fewer will go to college although they generally have made higher grades.[28] The ones who do have confidence enough for college will persist and a greater proportion of them will complete the baccalaureate program than will boys. Males outnumber females in most graduate programs. Evidence is in hand that many colleges and graduate schools have been systematically discriminating against female applicants by using different cut-off points on entrance tests or by applying quotas. There are proportionately fewer women among those receiving doctorates (13 percent) or law (10 percent) and medical (13 percent) degrees, considerably lower than in certain European countries such as West Germany and Russia.[29] Since most American young people could not finance such training alone, a major factor of discrimination in graduate work is that women receive only about 20 percent of all awards and fellowships, though certainly not because they are less qualified or do not apply.[30] Equally discouraging is the fact that millions of dollars are spent on male athletic programs, a fact currently being challenged by H.E.W. rulings.

It will be difficult, if not impossible, to change the self-image of women students until there are more women in higher education, so the problem resembles a vicious circle. A study of 1972-73 faculties indicated that women were only 22.5 percent of the 254,930 college professors in the nation and they were receiving almost $2,500 less in salaries.[31] Even with countless successful WEAL-supported cases on behalf of faculty women, by 1974 the salary differential was still $1,500 and sex was found to be a more persistent factor in discrimination than race.[32] Another part of the picture is the failure of institutions to promote women to the higher ranks; less than 10 percent of the women were full professors compared to 25.5 percent of the men.[33]

The prospects for changing the status quo for women in education began to be brighter in the early 70s. Courses in women's studies grew from 700 in 1971 to about 4,000 in 1974, and more than 350 universities and colleges were ordered under EO 11246 to eliminate discriminating circumstances. Within more than twenty of the professional organizations, caucuses and committees are taking a long, hard look at the status of women in their disciplines.[34]

The Christian, in assessing the educational differentials which perpetuate sexism throughout our society, needs to review the church literature for children, the sex distribution among the faculties of church schools and colleges, the need for women's studies, and the absence of church women in the governance of public and church-related schools. Denominations may yet see the time when the government will cite cases of discrimination in their recruitment of faculty, admissions of students, and salary schedules which could conceivably affect their tax-free and tax-deductible statuses.

The Media

The many faces of media offer an exciting array of possibilities for attitude change toward all oppressed and/or mythologized persons. Imagine what could be done with all the traditional nursery rhyme books if rewritten:[35]

Little Ms. Muffet
Sat on a tuffet,
Eating her burger and coke;
Along came a spider
And sat down beside her,
So she studied it under her
   microscope.

There was an old woman
Who lived in a shoe.
She had so many children
She said, "What shall we do?"
She found a good day-care,
The Pill, a job, too,
And made a down-payment
On a really big shoe.

Young boys, growing up in a preschool and early elementary school world that is overwhelmingly female, are most dependent on the secondary role models they find for "masculinity" in books and on TV. Textbooks with their definite role stereotyping, and especially history books with almost exclusively male heroes, have already been alluded to as a factor in early personality shaping. But a study of the toy sections of mail-order catalogs will show them divided carefully between girl and boy choices. Debbie can find bride dolls, makeup kits, and playhouses with simulated ovens and dishes; Bobby can choose from guns, speedboats, and construction kits.

Even the TV programs designed for children are dominated by males. "Sesame Street," often praised for its racial integration, has nevertheless been accused of sex role stereotyping. Note that most of the commercials on these programs are narrated by men and show them in persuasive, decisive roles. As they grow older, young people are quick to discern that almost all of the Ironsides and Kojaks are men, most of the medical heroes are male, and if they are fortunate enough to miss the daytime serials, they don't know that most of the people having troubles are women!

In the grown-up world, for years, women have been a sizeable contingent of some media, particularly journalism, but few have been "out front." Most women editors have covered the society section or religion and education. It would take more than one Barbara Walters to balance all the Julia Childs, Diana Shores, and Heloises. Women on newspapers have not varied much since 1950 (about 35 percent of all editorial personnel), but the magazines hire more women (45 percent of the professional employees) because women's magazines abound and women are concentrated there. A *Ms.* feature on the twelve top women news commentators on TV indicated that each of the three major networks has about 10 percent of its correspondents female. As indicated previously for women in politics, good looks, and a resonant voice are definite assets for women in communications.[36]

One of the prime targets for most women active in the liberation movement is the use of female stereotypes in commercial advertising. Curvy, sultry, bottle-blonds with far more makeup than the average woman in the kitchen or office would wear, proclaim the virtues of products from lawnmowers to men's aftershave lotions to liqueurs. If men are used to hawk wares, they are bruiser athletes, top-level executives, outdoor sportsmen, or rugged next-door types.

One might assume that in the popular music of contemporary youth, along with the protest of war, racism, and pollution would appear revolutionary images of women. A recent study of the lyrics of 197 contemporary recordings indicated the reverse was true: they were almost totally male-oriented, aggressive, and nonconforming. In almost every way the writers and the music industry for youth music have parroted all of the adult stereotypes for the sexes; indeed, women were of little concern to them![37]

Most of the churches' use of the media has been oriented toward the preaching ministry, which is obviously predominantly male. Only in the sacred music presented on radio and TV programs have women appeared in solo or choral performances. Only a few denominations have made much use of motion pictures, drama, or filmstrips and when they do, traditional sex roles are usually the norm. The media remains one of the greatest untapped resources for the church and women.

Conclusions

Institutional discrimination of women remains widespread, in spite of legal provisos for correcting the situation and many successful accomplishments of women in business, government, education, the media, and the churches. What concrete role can the Christian and the church play in this and other enterprises to help all people become full persons and participants in our society? For one thing, nothing speaks like example. The church and the denomination must recruit, employ, imburse, and appoint to serve, without consideration of factors other than ability and call. Too, by precept we must educate people about all issues of personhood wherever they occur in the institutions of society.

Notes

1. Quoted in the *San Francisco Chronicle Magazine,* July 26, 1970, p. 7.
2. Marijean Suelzle, "Women in Labor," *Transaction* 8, No. 1 & 2 (November-December, 1970), p. 54.
3. M. Barbara Boyle, "Equal Opportunities for Women Is Smart Business," *Harvard Business Review* 51, No. 3 (May, 1973), p. 86.
4. Abbott L. Ferris, *Indicators of Trends in the Status of American Women* (Russell Sage Foundation, 1971), p. 4.
5. "Wages and Women," *Time,* Vol. 103, No. 24 (June 17, 1974), p. 90.
6. U.S. Department of Labor data cited in Suelzle, *op. cit.,* p. 53.
7. *Time,* 99, No. 12 (March 20, 1972), p. 91.
8. Shirley Chisholm, "A Black Congresswoman Speaks Out for Women's Rights," Speech in U.S. House of Representatives, *Congressional Record,* 91st Congress, 1st Session, (May 21, 1969) 115:83, E4165-E4166.
9. Wyndham Robertson, "The Ten Highest Ranking Women in Big Business," *Fortune* LXXXVII, No. 4 (April, 1973), pp. 81 ff.
10. Time, *op. cit.,* pp. 38, 68, 81, 91.
11. Boyle, *op. cit.,* quoted p. 95.
12. *Ibid.,* p. 85.
13. *Ibid.,* p. 95.
14. Judith Neis, "The Abzug Campaign: A Lesson in Politics," *Ms.,* February, 1973, p. 77.
15. Paul Harvey, "The Women Are Coming," *Alexandria Daily Town Talk* (La.), May 24, 1974.
16. For fuller discussion of these problems, cf. Judith Anderson, "Sexual Politics: Chauvinism and Backlash?" *Today's Speech* 21, No. 4 (Fall, 1973), pp. 11-16.

17. Cited by Paul Harvey, *op. cit.*

18. Mary D. Keyserling, "Working Women Are Still Second," in Ann Scott, ed. *Women in American Life* (Houghton-Mifflin, 1970), pp. 178 ff.

19. Lorraine D. Eyde, "Status of Women in State and Local Government," *Public Personnel Management* 2 (May, 1973), p. 206.

20. Reported by Myra McPherson, syndicated by *The Washington Post*, printed in *Alexandria Daily Town Talk*, September 17, 1972.

21. *Time*, July 15, 1974, p. 33.

22. An excellent discussion of legislation re sexism is Kathryn G. Heath, "Legislation and Its Implications for Elimination of Sex Bias," *The Journal of the National Association for Women Deans, Administrators and Counselors*, 37: No. 2 (Winter, 1974), pp. 58-69.

23. *Time*, June 17, 1974, *op. cit.*

24. *Time*, March 20, 1972, *op. cit.*

25. *Ibid.*

26. Cited in Kirsten Amundsen, *The Silenced Majority: Women and American Democracy* (Englewood Cliffs, N.J.: Prentice-Hall, 1971), p. 215.

27. Myra and David Sadker, "Sexism in Schools: An Issue for the '70s" *Journal of the National Association for Women Deans, Administrators and Counselors, op. cit.*, p. 71.

28. M. Louise McBee and David E. Suddick, "Differential Freshman Admission by Sex," *Ibid.*, p. 75.

29. *Time*, March 20, 1972, pp. 38, 68, 81.

30. Cf. Cynthia L. Attwood, *Women in Fellowship and Training Programs* (Washington, D.C.: Association of American Colleges, November, 1972).

31. *Sex Discrimination*, (Washington, D.C.: U.S. Department of HEW, Office for Civil Rights, No. OCR 74-6), p. 2.

32. "On Campus with Women" (Washington, D.C.: Association of American Colleges) No. 3 (April, 1974), p. 10.

33. *Sex Discrimination, op. cit.*

34. "On Campus with Women" (Association of American Colleges) No. 1, (November, 1971), pp. 1-2.

35. The Walshes, "Letters," *Ms.* III, No. 1 (July, 1974), p. 7.

36. Judith Hennessee, "Ms. on the Arts," *Ms., op. cit.*, pp. 25 ff.

37. Cited in Janet S. Chafetz, *Masculine/Feminine or Human?* (F. E. Peacock, 1974), pp. 43-45.

8

Women and the Family in Today's World

Vera and David Mace

We have been looking in the previous chapters at some of the ways in which women's status and roles were seen in our Christian past. We have noted that the church did some good things *for* women, but also unfortunately did some bad things *to* women. We don't expect the church to be perfect. It is made up of human beings in all stages of Christian growth, and, inevitably, it has made many mistakes. In its attitude to women, however, the church faces as stern a challenge today as it has ever met in its entire history. Before we try to define that challenge, we must see just how it came about.

In order to do this, we must broaden our field of vision and look at the roles which men and women have played across the full sweep of human history, and in the many different cultures of the world. Of course this will have to be a very rough picture, painted in a few bold strokes on a broad canvas. But hopefully, it will give us the perspective we need to face the challenge of today. It will take the form of an overview of the roles and relationships of men and women in all the spheres in which they interact. We can identify a total of seven of these spheres:

Home and Family. As we have already seen, it is the biological differences between men and women that are the main determinants here, and motherhood is the key issue. Motherhood makes the woman vulnerable while she is pregnant and ties her to child-care obligations for many years thereafter. Traditionally, the father acted as protector and provider during these vulnerable years. Today, we are seeing a shift in these traditional roles as fathers and mothers begin to share the protecting and providing functions and at the same time also share the function of child-care which was assigned in the past to the mother.

Hunting and Fighting. Before agriculture was developed, hunting and fighting were essential for human survival. These are very active roles, and they tended to be reserved for men. It is true that the Roman goddess of hunting, Diana, was a woman. And it is true that the Greeks had a legend about a race of fighting women, the Amazons; but one of the disadvantages of being a woman appears in pictures of the fighting Amazons because the women concerned had had to cut off one of their breasts in order to wield a bow and arrow effectively. So, in general, hunting and fighting have among all peoples been almost universally considered as masculine roles.

Agriculture. As people learned to raise crops and to tame domestic animals, men and women for a time seem to have had almost equal roles. But there was always a tendency for men to prefer hunting and fighting, and to take the chance of leaving the women to do the work in the fields. Even among children who were learning their roles, the custom was for the boys to take care of the larger beasts—sheep, goats, cattle, and horses. David in the Bible, you will remember, was a shepherd boy. By contrast, the girls were sent to do weeding or to look after chickens.

Trade and Commerce. As men learned new skills, the things they produced began to be bought and sold. In this process of buying and selling, men and women were, at first, involved together. But as urban communities appeared and trade was increased, the men became the big operators, leaving the women to their home duties. Later, when large corporations developed in large cities, the men assumed the executive roles and women were pushed into the roles that involved less power and less responsibility.

Government. From the beginning, this was taken over almost exclusively by men. In the earliest organized social units, the chief functions of government were defense and the administration of justice. These roles appeared obviously to be male roles.

To deal with enemies and to cope with crimes required a strong man. So, women were largely left out. Although there were some significant exceptions, chiefs and councils of elders, rulers, and statesmen, and politicians, have almost always been men.

Religion. Most primitive peoples worshipped both gods and goddesses. As we have seen, this was true of the Greeks and Romans. But the Hebrew and Christian traditions were firmly monotheistic and patriarchal. God was thought of as a perfect example of the good father, the wise king, and the just judge. All of these were masculine roles. In the medieval Christian tradition, the Virgin Mary became an important figure and was in some measure worshipped, but this was the nearest approach in our entire history to any recognition of femininity associated with the godhead. In such a tradition, it was logical that women had little or no opportunity to serve as priests or pastors.

Education. All peoples have had some system of preparing and training young people for adult life. At first, this was based on learning the simple elements of tribal lore. Almost from the beginning, we can find a division of educational patterns as boys and girls were prepared for their particular masculine and feminine roles. Usually the boys were trained by the father, the girls by the mother. Where there were initiation ceremonies at puberty, these stressed separate sex roles, or they were confined to boys only. In the Jewish communities, over long periods of time, education was entirely religious, and exclusively for boys. In more recent times, with the development of public schools, basic education has not distinguished between boys and girls. But as they grew older, there tended to be subjects that were appropriate for girls, and others appropriate for boys; behind all this was the basic concept that boys were trained for careers and girls for homemaking. Even when training for careers was available to girls, the kind and number of these careers was strictly limited.

This brief sketch will show that, almost universally in human societies, there was a fairly strict differentiation of masculine and feminine roles, involving a differentiation of status. At first, these differences were appropriate ways of conveniently dividing up the duties that had to be performed, and men and women in simple communities tended to work side by side.

Peasant families worked together to cultivate their piece of land, and the children of both sexes shared as soon as they were able. Traders sold their goods at their front door, or in a simple shop that was just part of the house. Craftsmen had their workshops in the home. In Old Testament times, religious ceremonies were a central part of homelife, and although the husband presided, the wife did her part by making preparation and helping to teach the children how to play their assigned roles.

As towns and cities developed and grew larger, however, the home became more and more isolated from the real life of the community. The fighting man, who in the past had been concerned with defending his homestead from attackers, was now drafted into an army and often went off to distant places for long periods of time. The father who had formerly worked at home now went off to his place of business in the town, often commuting long distances by road or rail. Religious ceremonies moved out of the home and focused in the synagogue or the church. Government moved from the council of village elders to full-time chiefs and kings, and then involved large numbers of politicians and statesmen.

Most of these changes have come gradually at first, but their effect has been progressively to shift the focus of community life—the place "where the action is"—further and further away from the home. This has reached its extreme point in the big cities of today, with the family home isolated in the suburbs, and the father away all day, while the children are at school or in kindergarten or occupied in the evening with activities planned for them alone.

By this time, the woman was being increasingly deprived of any real part in the significant life of the world in which she lived. She bore children, but fewer of them than before, which shortened the period in which she was occupied with child-care.

But although she had more free time, her role seemed less and less important as breakfast cereals, packaged meals, and school lunches deprived her of her function as provider of meals. She was no longer needed to make or mend clothes, to bottle fruit, to prescribe medicine, to entertain or teach her children. She was no longer expected, either, to counsel with her husband about his farm management or business affairs. She did no work that was considered useful enough to be paid for. Her opinions were not sought about any important decisions affecting the life of the community. She was educated, but what for? She now lived in a culture where a person's value was increasingly recognized by being paid a wage, by being given a job. In such a setting, she sometimes felt no more important than a pet canary in a gilded cage.

So women today have finally revolted. The anger and frustration and humiliation that have long simmered silently in their hearts have come to the boil, and they are now demanding a real place in the real world. Some of their actions may seem wild and irresponsible; but they live in an age in which you have to take extreme measures in order to be either seen or heard. Few of them are really extremists. They don't want to tear the world apart. They don't want to take over the government. They don't even want to compete with men. What they want is recognition of their personhood, and a fair and equitable restructuring of human affairs that will give them a voice in the important decisions, a hand in the big enterprises, and the respect to which they feel entitled as intelligent, responsible, and competent members of the human community. They want a complete and objective reevaluation of the roles of men and women in the new kind of human society we are creating today; and it seems clear that they aren't going to settle for less.

What has happened is that a crisis which has been developing for long centuries has now caught up with us, and we must face it, because it isn't going to go away. This crisis reaches into every area of our common life. And that includes the church. Indeed, it very specially concerns the church, because the claim is being widely made that religion has been one of the strongest influences in denying woman a right to full personhood. Our purpose in this book is to examine that accusation as fairly and as honestly as we can; hopefully to gain some new insights; and to try to decide what action, if any, needs to be taken.

Homemaking in Our Modern World

We must now move from the broad picture to a more concentrated one. Let us try to see what today's woman is up against when she marries and starts a family. We will make a balance sheet of the positive and negative factors involved.

On the positive side, today's homemaker lives in an economy of abundance. In these days we are all complaining about inflation, and it is indeed a distressing problem. But in full perspective, it becomes clear that to Americans it is no more than a minor nuisance. It would take a great deal of inflation to scale American living standards down to the levels at which people have managed to live throughout human history, and even to the levels at which most people in the world today still live. There was a recent case history given on television, describing a married couple with an income of $12,000 a year, who were in trouble because they had used up all their savings and had to seek financial counseling. The counseling revealed that they had gone into the red as a result of buying a clothes dryer. Now, it is a simple fact that most people in the world would never dream of the possibility of owning a clothes dryer. They would simply hang up the clothes on a line and let them dry. So, it is a fact that today's young woman in America begins her homemaking under almost ideal conditions, with more than adequate resources. In most cases, she has a comfortable house or apartment, lavishly furnished and equipped, and has access to plenty of good food. Though she has no household help, she has machines that take most of the drudgery out of housework.

This is the great gift which technology has provided for the modern woman, and it is an achievement we may be proud of. Following World War II, when homes were scarce and young couples often had to double up with inlaws, the dream of the average American young woman was to have a modern house or apartment, in a pleasant suburban development, where she could devote herself through the years to raising her 3.7 children. That dream has now been almost fully realized. But, to the consternation of the planners, the dream has turned into a nightmare. Instead of being grateful and contented, millions of American homemakers are suffering from what Margaret Mead has called the "trapped housewife syndrome."

What has happened? In order to find out, we must look at the negative side of the balance sheet. We can conveniently divide up the areas of family life under four headings—homemaking, parenthood, child-raising, and marriage.

Homemaking. The plain truth is that running a household was once an art, and is no longer so. Skills that were required in bygone times have all been taken over commercially. All the products which the housewife's hands shaped and prepared may now be purchased over the counter. Even if she is not satisfied with run-of-the-mill goods, she can have whatever she wants "custom made" to her own specifications. There are no significant skills or crafts that give the average married woman a sense of personal pride and achievement. Indeed, the very term "home-made" now suggests something that is poorly constructed and even shoddy. Of course, there are still imaginative and gifted women who make their own bread, buy old furniture and refinish it, excel in needlework, and so on. But this brings only very limited fulfillment to them, and little praise from their neighbors. We must face the fact that the rewards of homemaking have greatly diminished.

Parenthood. The injunction in the Bible was to "be fruitful and multiply." The implication was that having plenty of children was a valuable contribution to the community. Today this is reversed, and the production of many children offers the most serious threat that exists to our human future. This has radically changed our whole estimate of child-bearing. In the days of the Roman Empire, the Roman legions marching to war habitually saluted a pregnant woman. They were risking their lives for their country, and so was she. This high praise for the woman who bore children has dominated history until the present time. Multitudes of artists have painted pictures of a mother and child, and no subject in the realm of art has been more popular. Motherhood was a woman's crowning glory.

Not any more. The talk now is of "zero population growth," which means two children, at most, as the tolerated limit. There are young people, and even organizations of young people, who believe that it is best these days to have no children at all. The childless marriage was once an object of compassion and pity to the friends of the couple concerned. Now it is often considered an evidence of high idealism on the part of the couple. It is no doubt still true, and always will be, that a woman finds deep biological and psychological fulfillment in bearing a child. But it is no longer true that this necessarily inflates her ego and builds up her self-esteem. The opposite may be nearer the truth.

Child-Raising. In the old days, raising children was comparatively easy. Strict discipline commanded obedience; so, rebellion was not very frequent. Anyway, women bearing many children simply couldn't give much individual attention to them, and in large families they tended to bring up each other. Often, too, household help was available. If a child was particularly troublesome and badly behaved, the mother was not blamed but pitied. The assumption was that there was something inherently wrong with the child. Some evil spirit or other malevolent influence was at work, defeating all the best efforts of the devoted parents. Sympathy was extended to the parents of such children, and if the situation became really bad, the accepted thing was for the parents to renounce the child altogether, and let him go his wayward, wicked way.

Freud changed all that. Now, if a child grows up disturbed or delinquent, this is at once attributed to some deficiency in the parents. The mother, in particular, feels the accusing finger pointed at her. So, young mothers avidly read books on child psychology, anxiously watch the behavior of their children, debate with each other the latest magazine article on the best pattern of discipline, argue about the respective merits of firmness and permissiveness. The ultimate implication behind all this is that to be a really effective mother one should have a graduate degree in child development. Since this is out of the reach of the average mother, she labors under a continuing sense of incompetence.

But she is soon aware of further complications. Even if the mother of today is confident about her capacity to raise her children properly, she often doesn't get a chance to do so. As Margaret Mead has put it, many parents stand helpless and frustrated while the mass media raise their children! Catholics used to claim that if you did the right things for a child during its first seven years, there would be little likelihood of trouble after that. But in today's world, the TV gets into the process long before the child is seven, and may negate the best efforts of the parents to put him on the right path. Then the public schools take over, and throw him into close contact with other children who, in a pluralistic society, may have been raised with totally different values than those of his parents. By the time he has become a teenager, the youth culture takes over and assiduously teaches him to defy his parents and to "do his own thing." So child-raising, which used to be considered a rich and rewarding experience for the mother, has progressively become so anxiety-producing that many women feel profoundly thankful if they can get through it without a nervous breakdown!

Marriage. The one thing that would help the woman most to overcome all these frustrations would be the warm, dependable, supportive love of her husband; but she can no longer count on this. American men have been walking out on their wives, on an increasing scale, since the beginning of this century. During most of that time American divorce rates have been the highest in the world. The hope was that wives would, in time, become more skilled at what some women's magazines called "holding your man." But it hasn't turned out that way. Instead, under the influence of the women's liberation movement, wives have now started leaving their husbands in much the same way as husbands used to leave their wives. This has been made much easier than before by the passing of no-fault divorce laws in more and more states. The national average is now approaching fifty divorces for every hundred new marriages in a given year, and we now have no less than twelve million one-parent families in North America. In the great majority of these families, it is the mother who is the one parent. If raising children in a two-parent family is anxiety-producing, in a one-parent family all the difficulties are greatly increased.

These disturbing events are leading women more and more to what seems an inevitable conclusion. Girls in American culture have long been led to believe that the way to deep and enduring fulfillment is to get married and live happily ever after. They have taken this on trust, and gone on believing it. But the mounting mass of evidence to the contrary has finally shattered the dream, and this has led to a reaction of deep disillusionment and bitterness. In some of its more extreme forms, the Women's Liberation Movement has blamed marriage and the family for the enslavement of women through the ages and has encouraged its members to renounce marriage and motherhood in the struggle to gain their freedom. Clare Booth Luce, who is by no means an extremist, has described marriage as the most male dominated of all our institutions. As she has expressed it: "It is the only institution in which women are expected to work without any stipulated wages and with no fixed working hours."

It is indeed a strange spectacle to witness women turning against family life. Throughout the whole of recorded history, women have been easily persuaded that homemaking is the greatest fulfillment that this life has to offer them, and many have found it so. Is this no longer true today? Evidently not.

Drawing on a number of research findings, Dr. Jessie Bernard, one of our leading family sociologists, demonstrates in her book, *The Future of Marriage,* that when we compare the mental and emotional health of married men and women, the wives are decidedly more likely to suffer from feelings of anxiety, inadequacy, and depression than their husbands, and more likely to commit suicide. In other words, marriage today is much better and healthier for men than for women. Of course, the question could be asked whether women are in any case much more subject to these mental disturbances. But this does not seem to be so. The record for the emotional and mental health of *married* women turns out to be decidedly worse than for *unmarried* women. In other words, life is better in general today for a woman who doesn't marry than for one who does. Obviously, we don't know, and never will know, whether this was also true in the past. But it *is* true now.

We are well aware that we have drawn a very negative picture. We have done so deliberately. These are grim facts, but they must be faced. To dismiss the problem of woman's status and roles by declaring haughtily that woman's place is in the home, and that she had better come to her senses and go back to where she belongs, only reveals gross ignorance of the true facts. And it will achieve absolutely nothing, because the situation has now been radically changed in two important ways. First, women have finally achieved what is called ESE—economic, sexual, and educational liberation. They are no longer going to do what men tell them to do, but only what they themselves judge to be best. And secondly, the nature of marriage and family life has also been radically altered in our time so that the kind of home in which women in the past found fulfillment is rapidly going out of existence altogether. Consequently, the old fulfillments that were offered to women in homemaking are, in many cases, no longer there.

There is, of course, a positive answer to all this; and it will be our task to try to present it in the next chapter.

9

Women, Men, and Marriage

Vera and David Mace

Having confronted the disturbing and challenging situation of modern women's status and roles, we must now try to see what can be done about it. We will begin by summarizing the problem from a rather different angle.

In our highly developed modern societies, we are forced to live in two separate worlds. We often call them the private sector and the public sector. On a visit to the Soviet Union, we went to see a child-care center, and found very small children crawling around together in the same playpen. The worker explained to us that Russians believe it is good for children to start very young in learning to interact with each other. In this way, from the begining, they learn the collective way of life. We sometimes express this by saying that we must each learn to be a big frog in a small pool, and a small frog in a big pool. Both of these worlds—the intimate one of the home, and the more impersonal world outside—are meaningful and important to us. We need to be able to function in both in order to live a truly fulfilled life. Anyone confined to only one world is a deprived person. For example, a man holding an important job but without a home, is deprived of the intimacy, and support, and relaxation that home provides. A woman secure in her home, but without any really significant role outside the home, is deprived of the opportunity to express and use many of her aptitudes and gifts.

In earlier times, when life was simple, these two worlds were not significantly separated. People lived in relatively small, close-knit kinship groups, in which the family and the tribe were in continual interaction. But as urban society became more and more complex, these two worlds were stretched further and further apait. We might say that they became polarized. And the distance between them has become progressively greater and greater, so that today it could run into many miles, as in the case of the man who commutes between his office in the big city and his home in the outlying suburb. We once lived in a New Jersey community, twenty-five miles from New York City, and men who worked in the big city told us that on week days they hardly ever saw their young children. They left home early in the morning before the children were up, and returned in the evening after the children had gone to bed.

Despite these hardships, men in our culture have managed to enjoy living in both worlds. It is the women who have been more and more deprived. Generation after generation, they have been further and further cut off from participation in the larger world, and denied any real share either in its tasks or its rewards. This has been made particularly frustrating during the present century, as women, in increasing numbers, have had the chance of a good education. They have been encouraged as responsible citizens to take an intelligent interest in what was going on around them—to read newspapers, magazines, and books; to hear and often to meet interesting people who are engaged in important enterprises; to learn skills that could contribute to meeting human needs or to advancing human progress. In other words, they have been educated and trained in very much the same way as men are. And then, just when they reached maturity and were all ready to go, they found themselves shunted into marriage and motherhood, switched off the main track and stuck in a sideline while their men went rolling on and left them far behind.

Some women have not been unduly bothered about all this. Perhaps they weren't very ambitious, or they were very happily married, or they believed it was their duty to stay in the small private world of the home and make the best of it. But for more and more women the whole situation has led to frustration and a keen sense of injustice. Why, they complained, should men, and only men, have the best of both worlds?

A number of factors have encouraged women in this direction. One was that during both World Wars, when the men went away to fight, the women took over and kept the country going—and did it so well that they proved that they were just as competent as men. Another factor was that the cutting down of the number of children in the average family, combined with the great increase in life expectancy, gave the average married woman a long stretch of years in which she was not occupied with child-care duties, and running a home took up only a fraction of her time. These women began to move in increasing numbers into paid employment; and they found that they liked it. Not only did it give them financial independence, but they were particularly fulfilled in being part of the workaday world, and not just spectators. They found their self-esteem raised and they lost the feeling that they were second-class citizens.

But there was a price to pay for all this. With both men and women heavily involved in the public world, the private world began to suffer. When husband and wife are spending as much as ten hours a day getting to work, working, and then getting home again, what happens to family life? One thing is that the housework doesn't get done. And there isn't much time either, for those long, leisurely hours of mutual sharing of thoughts and feelings—for all the intimate experiences that nourish and sustain a marriage. And when the marriage doesn't get nourished, a slow, subtle process of drifting apart can easily set in. Needs unmet in the marriage relationship begin to be met outside the marriage. Then husband and wife start to deceive each other and to avoid each other, and a crisis of some kind soon develops. When this happens, the couple may not have the time, the resources, or the motivation to struggle with it and resolve it. And so, before long, another marriage is headed for the divorce court, another group of children must face painful and complex processes of readjustment, and another family unit collapses into a pile of human wreckage.

As we have already seen, the new factor in divorce today is that the wife is taking the initiative more and more often. There was a time when a wife would put up with almost anything to hold her marriage together, because her economic security and her status in the community were both at stake. Nowadays, this has greatly changed. Marriage counselors are reporting many cases in which the wife, strongly influenced by the women's liberation movement, decides that her marriage is denying her personal growth and freedom. So she begins to take a tough line with her husband, demanding that he make all kinds of adjustments and concessions. The husband is outraged to find his wife challenging his authority, and, after a few half-hearted attempts to be conciliatory, he fights back. With no one really trying to save the marriage, and with divorce so easy to get, a separation soon follows. Then later, when it is all over, the wife may discover that instead of being exhilerated by her new-found freedom, she is lonely, frightened, and emotionally exhausted. She faces the difficult task of having to start life all over again and trying to be both mother and father to her uprooted children. Many of these women go through very traumatic experiences. Sooner or later, of course, most of them remarry; and, if the second marriage brings them real fulfillment, all the suffering may in the end seem worthwhile. But too often the new marriage isn't really any better than the old one could have been if it had been better managed.

So what? Are we advocating that women should put up with anything in order to stay married? Are we saying that *any* kind of marriage is better than *no* marriage? That sounds like endorsing the very policy that has enabled men to dominate and exploit their wives, and has created the present crisis.

At this point we must stop and face the fact that, in the end, there can be no solution to the problems of the modern woman that does not involve the modern man. We have a great deal of sympathy with the predicament of women today. We think their problems are real. We think they have suffered, and still suffer, many injustices. We think they are entitled to state their case, and to ask for radical changes in many of our traditional attitudes. But we don't think they are going to make really significant progress by adopting the policy of attacking men as though they were their natural enemies. A great battle between the sexes would hurt a lot of people, and in the end it wouldn't achieve much. The greatest hope for ultimate success is for women to persuade men to be their allies and to work with them. We think this can be done if women go about it in the right way. Women have great power over men, from infancy to old age. We believe that their best strategy would be to use this power, both in and out of marriage, to achieve their legitimate goals.

We don't think the women's movement in this country has seen this clearly enough. It has often adopted an aggressive, belligerent strategy. Up to a point, this was perhaps necessary, because in these days of extremism you have to do something dramatic to get a hearing. But we think the women have now been heard very clearly, and the time has come for men and women to work together for their mutual liberation. Some men would resist the idea that they need to be liberated, but it is nevertheless true. Men in our culture have a great many advantages over women. They hold most of the power in their hands. But they also work under tremendous strain, and carry crippling burdens of responsibility. They are driven by relentless urges to succeed, to measure up to standards that don't make sense, to keep up a show of authority and strength and assertiveness that isn't really necessary. The culture compels them to conform to a concept of masculinity that is just as spurious as the baby-doll image of femininity that women of today have so indignantly repudiated.

So let's see how men and women could work together to make family life function more effectively in today's world. We're quite convinced that it can be done. In recent years, we have been deeply involved in the marriage enrichment movement, and we have been greatly encouraged to see many a couple take a good hard look at their traditional marriage, reach agreement about how they want to restructure it, go to work together, and in time develop a much more satisfying relationship.

In order to reach this highly desirable objective, we must make it possible for married couples to achieve five goals:

1. *Accept the concept of companionship marriage.* One of our greatest American family sociologists, Ernest W. Burgess, published in 1945 a book entitled *The Family: From Institution to Companionship.* In this book he defined the radical changes taking place in the family today. We quote what he and his co-author, Harvey Locke, said in the preface to the book: "Our central thesis is that the family in historical times has been, and at present is, in transition from an institution to a companionship. In the past the important factors unifying the family have been external, formal, and authoritarian, as the law, the mores, public opinion, tradition, the authority of the family head, rigid discipline, and elaborate ritual. At present, in the new emerging form of the companionship family, its unity inheres less and less in community pressures and more and more in such inter-personal relationships as the mutual affection, the sympathetic understanding, and the comradeship of its members."

Anyone who has observed modern families closely will agree that this exactly describes what is taking place. You may not like this kind of change, but whether you like it or not, nothing can alter the fact that it is happening.

However, we like it. We believe it not only offers us families that can function more effectively in our world of today, but families that are better, happier, and healthier than most have been in the past. It is important, however, to understand that we can have these better families only by working for them. We'll come back to that later.

At the heart of the companionship family is the companionship marriage. And since this confronts us as Christians with a critical question, let's face it right away. The question is this: Is Christian marriage a hierarchy or a partnership?

What would be your answer? Let us spell it out clearly. Is the husband/wife relationship for Christians like the relationship between master and slave, between employer and employee? Or is it like the relationship between cooperating partners, between friends or companions? Think it over carefully—it is a vitally important question. You can't give both answers. You must choose one or the other.

Let's go back to the Bible. The book of Genesis tells us that God established marriage for three reasons—for children, for sex, and for mutual aid. These three reasons are stated in the wedding ritual of most Christian churches.

All right, let's take them one by one. First, will father and mother function best together on a master/servant basis, or on a partnership basis? There could be some argument about this one. We personally favor the parents cooperating as partners and reaching decisions together by negotiation. You may favor the heavy-handed father making the decisions and the wife meekly accepting them. Okay.

The second reason for marriage is to provide sexual fulfillment. Does the husband demand sex whenever he wants it, and the wife offer her body submissively in response? (The church has supported this latter view in its insistence on the husband's "marriage rights.") Or is sex something mutual they agree about together?

The third reason for marriage is to aid and support each other. The Bible says that Eve was to be a "help meet" for Adam. How do you interpret this? Was Eve a sort of employee, like a plumber's assistant? Or was she a cooperating companion? We personally favor the companionship concept. But you may prefer the other.

So where do we come out? We may have to agree to disagree. Clearly there are passages in the Bible that support the hierarchical concept—the text about Adam "ruling over Eve," and what Paul said about wives "submitting" to their husbands. But there are other passages that equally support the companionship concept. We've already referred to some of them. We think that the weight of evidence in the Bible supports the companionship marriage. You may think otherwise. What is important, though, is that *you can't say that the Bible supports one view and denounces the other.* We really have a choice.

We once spent twelve weeks in northern Thailand with a group of twenty, picked, Asian Christian leaders studying this very question. The traditional Asian marriage pattern clearly favors the master/slave relationship between husband and wife. Some of our group argued that when they became Christians, they didn't have to change. They could still boss their wives around and the Bible would support them in this. But as we got deeper into the Bible teaching, this view didn't stand up. We finally agreed that the Bible doesn't impose on us *any* particular pattern of marriage, just as it doesn't insist on a particular educational philosophy or a particular form of government. What the Bible is concerned with is that husbands and wives should be loving and caring toward each other. When our Asians saw this clearly, they gave in. They knew very well that if husbands loved their wives, as Christ loved the church, they couldn't boss them around anymore.

Notice that in this discussion we have never used the word "equality." When it is used to describe marriage, it is an inappropriate, irrelevant, misleading word. How *could* two people who marry each other be equal? Equal in what? In the whole wide range of activities they share together? That could never happen. In every marriage, there are some things the husband can do better than the wife and some things the wife can do better than the husband. And if they are good companions, they will soon share the responsibilities on the basis of who does which job better.

The important word is not "equality" but "equity." This word means "fairness." It means that husband and wife both *share* in their joint life. Each has a fair share of the goodies, and each accepts a fair share of the chores. That's what true companions always do when they work together. When the other's burden gets too heavy, you say, "Look, let me take a turn."

That's equity—and equity is the word that describes the companionship marriage. Surely every Christian married couple should be companions in that sense.

2. Shift from fixed roles to shared roles. We've been hearing a lot about the "sexual revolution." Now we are beginning to hear about the "sex role" revolution!

We remember reading about a big industrial dispute that held up the construction of a New York skyscraper. It all began because an electrician refused to bore a hole through a wall. He had a drill and he could easily have done it. But he argued that this was a job for a carpenter. There wasn't a carpenter around, so the foreman told the electrician to go ahead and drill the hole anyway. He still refused, and appealed to his union for support. Next thing, all the electricians walked off the job!

That's what we mean by roles. And in traditional marriages there were the husband's roles and the wife's roles. Husbands earned the money to bring home the bacon, and did a few technical jobs around the house; wives took care of the home and the children. No self-respecting husband would change a baby's diapers, and no self-respecting wife would replace a burned-out fuse. Of course, you say, we've given up all that nonsense today. But have we? Just read the story of the first eight days of the marriage of John and Sue in chapter 3 of the best-selling book *Open Marriage,* by Nena and George O'Neill, and see how role expectations, reinforced by unconscious prejudice, can in one week get a loving couple tied up in knots. It's a painful business for husband and wife to sit down and examine honestly and fairly the role expectations they are imposing on one another. But if they do it as loving companions, it can set them free from a whole mass of unkind and critical judgments that could otherwise seriously damage their relationship.

In good marriages today the roles are flexible. Indeed, they are shared. There are now very few behaviors that are okay for men but not for women, or okay for women and not for men. There are no tasks that are exclusive to the husband's union or to the wife's union. the well-being of the family is what matters, and who does what must be decided with that as the goal. The wise rule is expressed in the old saying, "From each according to his ability; to each according to his need." Maybe it is even better expressed by an adaptation of the "Golden Rule" to married couples, "Do for your marriage partner what you would like your marriage partner to do for you."

3. *Learn the art of interpersonal competence.* We first came across this term in the book *Identity and Interpersonal Competence* by Cottrell and Foote, published in 1955. It is the key to the sex role revolution. Let us explain.

The traditional type of marriage was like a play for which the actors were carefully prepared in advance. For years they had learned their parts. The word "role" is derived from a French word meaning the script which an actor learns by heart. Boys, during the years they were being raised, learned the proper roles of a man, of a husband. They learned that it is not manly to play with dolls, because a real husband doesn't take care of babies. They learned that it is not manly to admit you are wrong, or that you made a mistake, because a good husband is never wrong. Girls, in the same way, learned the roles appropriate for a wife. They learned that it isn't womanly to handle tools, because doing things with wood and metal is not a suitable occupation for wives. They learned that it isn't womanly to be angry, because wives are always sweet and patient. And so on. By the time they were old enough to marry, the boys and girls knew exactly how to behave toward each other, and the play went on smoothly and precisely as long as the husband and wife didn't depart from the script, and as long as they didn't allow their deeper feelings as people to get in the way.

But one of the discoveries of our time is that marriage is much better when people really are their true selves and really share their true feelings with each other. Much better, yes; but unfortunately, also much more difficult. The reason why most couples give up trying to be companions is that they just don't know how. The average husband is ham-handed and helpless when he is confronted by his wife's real emotions; so she learns to bottle them up, and he learns not to ask her about her deeper thoughts and feelings and not to tell her about his. Since their attempts to achieve intimacy produce alarming results, they back up and settle for a superficial relationship. Then, because a superficial relationship isn't really satisfying and isn't really what they wanted, they become disillusioned and drift apart. This is a pretty good description of how millions of American marriages get onto the rocks.

Supposing there was a way of teaching married couples not to be afraid of their own and each other's deeper feelings. Supposing we could really *train* couples to be true companions, and to enter into depth relationships with each other? Well, we have to tell you it *is* possible. We *can* do it. In fact, this is the way to enable men and women today to make companionship marriages work—just as training in the stereotyped sex roles was the way to make traditional marriages work. At the heart of most broken marriages today lies the fact that what people want is companionship marriage; but they can't make this work because they have been trained for traditional marriage. It's as if we trained an athlete carefully for the hundred-yard dash, and then he found himself entered for the high jump!

This may sound almost absurd—yet it is actually true. We are either giving people training for a type of marriage which they don't want; or, just as often nowadays, we are giving them no training for marriage at all. Either way, they just aren't prepared for the difficult and complex tasks of the companionship marriage, which means encountering each other as persons, accepting each other as they really are, and working together to achieve all the fulfillments of the shared life. this is a task so difficult that it can't be done without learning the skills that give people interpersonal competence. Unfortunately, we haven't space to tell you in detail what these skills are, but they include effective couple communication; the capacity to express and accept each other's true feelings, positive and negative; the capacity to use conflict constructively; and the capacity to resolve the deadly love-anger cycle. In the past few years, behavioral scientists have made important and exciting progress in the understanding of these critical areas of the marriage relationship.

Perhaps it is little wonder that some Christians cling rather desperately to the traditional, hierarchical pattern of marriage. After all, it avoids a lot of hard work and painful adjustment for the husband to claim that God made him a superior being and that therefore his wife must treat him as such. And when he is confronted with the statement, "There is neither male nor female. We are all one in Christ Jesus," no doubt he can think of some clever interpretation that will explain it away.

Unfortunately, however, there are going to be fewer and fewer such husbands, for the simple reason that there are going to be fewer and fewer wives who are prepared to accept the statement that God made the woman an inferior being. So perhaps we had better get into this business of interpersonal competence and find out what it is all about.

4. *Sharing work and responsibility.* Once the husband and wife have been delivered from the tyranny of role expectations, they can begin to work out a way of living the shared life that is right for them. This is very exciting and very rewarding. They must begin by really getting to know each other; and if you say that two people can't live together in marriage without getting to know each other, we can testify, on the basis of forty years of marriage counseling, that this is very far from the truth. We could give you case histories of husbands and wives who were so successful in concealing their true selves from each other, and in failing to see each other as they really were, that if a written description of the inner life of one of them were to be presented to the other, it would be totally unrecognizable. It is often said that love is blind. Perhaps the opposite is nearer the truth. Only people who truly love each other really get to know each other. It is suspicion, hostility, and rejection that

make people blind.

Once two married people really know each other, they can plan intelligently how they will operate their shared life. This means allocating duties and responsibilities, not on the basis of what the traditional roles prescribe but on the basis of what gifts and qualifications the partners possess. If the husband is hopeless at keeping records and can't add up figures accurately, he could, of course, learn to do better; but in the meantime, if his wife is good at performing both of these operations, it would surely make sense for her to manage the family finances. If the wife's judgment about interior decorating is poor, but the husband has a good eye for design and a good color sense, is there any reason why he shouldn't plan the furnishings of the home? Once this sensible way of making decisions is arrived at, real progress can be made. As to work that both can do equally well, it can either be divided up between them, or the jobs can be allocated to one or the other, or they can take turns on alternate days or alternate weeks.

It is by this kind of planning of work and responsibility that the great principle of *equity* is put into practice. There are things that have to be done in a family that no one likes to do. Nothing humiliates a marriage partner more than to be expected to do an unfair share of these unpleasant chores. This is perhaps the only area in marriage where the principle of equality should be strictly applied.

In more and more marriages these days, the couple face the question: Should the wife go out to work? Obviously there is no general rule that can be applied to *all* couples; so, this question must be dealt with on a personal basis. The important thing to remember is that this question always can be settled by mutual agreement if the husband and wife really see their relationship as one of companionship, if they love and respect each other, and if they have agreed to manage their affairs on the principle of equity. When stubborn differences occur between husband and wife concerning the wife's right to work outside the home, these differences almost always reflect the failure of the couple to build a good relationship in other areas. Any husband and wife, who really care about each other, will obviously settle this question on the basis of what is best for all concerned; for each of them, for their children, and for the welfare of their family. A wife who has to assert her right to take a job against her husband's stubborn opposition, in circumstances that leave her children neglected or uncared for, is being forced to fight a battle in one area and lose out in other areas. People who love, trust, and respect each other just don't do this kind of thing to each other.

5. *Becoming more effective parents.* The task of parenthood has probably never been more demanding than it is in our world of today. We have seen how attempts of parents to provide their children with sound guidelines for living are constantly interrupted by conflicting voices from the outside world which suggest entirely different rules. We have seen how, in a pluralistic society, growing children and adolescents have freedom to choose, and in addition, a variety of choices that simply didn't exist in the stable, monolithic societies of the past. In this exasperating situation, what can parents do?

We are quite sure that the most important thing they can do is to give their children *love*—warm, outgoing love, if possible with no strings attached. But unfortunately there is a prior condition that has to be met before such love can be given. Parents can't love their children in a healthy, mature way unless they love one another. The kind of love that provides the perfect setting for the healthy emotional development of a child is the product of the warm, abundant, joyous love which father and mother have for each other. Without this, there is danger that a parent, consciously or unconsciously, may try to use the relationship with the child to meet his or her own unmet needs for love.

What this means is that the key to effective parenthood is effective marriage, and we are deeply convinced of this. It is very seldom that parents who have a really deep relationship of love and trust for each other have serious trouble with their children. And there is no more fundamental way in which a man and woman can forge the best kind of companionship with each other than in devoting themselves together, for the joy and fulfillment it gives them, to the welfare of their children. For such couples, even in these difficult days, raising children can still be an experience of sheer delight.

Another important aspect of successful parenthood is, once again, the companionship relationship. Burgess didn't just speak of the companionship *marriage*—he referred to the whole family as functioning on a companionship basis. And everything we have said about our poor training for marriage is equally true of our poor training for parenthood. Here, too, we have been trained for parental roles that no longer work in today's world.

The traditional concept of the parents' role was to take a piece of plastic clay and shape it into a mature human being. This meant discipline and indoctrination. The parents were all-wise and all-knowing, and the child had to accept unconditionally what the parents said, and obey the parents' demands. We have swung to the opposite extreme and tried to raise our children on a doctrine of almost complete permissiveness that borders on unrestricted indulgence. It is as if we had begun by strapping the child tightly to an upright pole until he could hardly move, and then suddenly had untied him and set him loose with no support whatever so that he tumbled about all over the place.

The only effective way to raise children today is by cooperation—winning the child's friendship and trust and then working with him as he learns by experimenting; feeding him freedom as long as he is able to handle it responsibly, gently restraining him when he tends to misuse freedom by hurting himself and others. This way works like a charm; but it can only work when the parents can maintain a real companionship relationship with their children. Many parents, alas, seem to have neither the time nor the inclination to stay with it. Yet by doing the job right, they would in the end save themselves time and be spared a great deal of possible heartache and disillusionment.

Of course there is much to learn about parenthood. Yet the basic ground rules are really quite simple, and it isn't really necessary to study the big books on child development in order to succeed. Relatively short courses on parent effectiveness have been very helpful in putting many married couples on the right track.

Conclusion

We have chosen in this chapter to talk about the needs of women in the context of the liberation of both men and women together. We believe that this is the only way. To try to change the conditions of life for half the human race without the cooperation of the other half is an impossible undertaking. This is particularly true of marriage and the family, but it is true also of the shared life of men and women in the wider world, which was once almost exclusively the domain of men but in which women are now joining them in large numbers.

Indeed, it is our conviction that only when the full partnership of men and women is realized in marriage will it also come about in the wider world. Let us conclude by quoting what we have said about this in our book, *We Can Have Better Marriages If We Really Want Them:*

It would seem to us that the true comradeship between men and women which we seek will not be fully achieved outside marriage until it is achieved in marriage, and that once it is achieved extensively in marriage, its achievement outside marriage will be inevitable. What, after all, is holding back the cause of women's liberation? Mainly the stubborn opposition of men, who, unwilling to accept an equal comradeship with their wives at home, therefore fear its implications in the wider life of the nation. And what, more than anything else, will change their minds? The discovery in their marriage that a wife no longer discriminated against becomes not a rampaging renegade, but a loyal partner and a trusted friend.

10
Women and the Sexual Revolution

Harry N. Hollis, Jr.

The real sexual revolution is the emergence of women from passivity, from thingness, to full self-determination, to full dignity. And insofar as they can do this, men are also emerging from the stage of identification with brutality and masters to full and sensitive and complete humanity.—Betty Friedan [1]

When a man marries a female rather than a woman the marriage is in grave danger, and the same is true when a woman marries a male rather than a man. The extent to which sex can destroy personal relations is an evidence of the importance of sex in personal relations.—Vancouver Study Group [2]

Has there been a sexual revolution? Serious students of American behavior are debating the answer to this question. Meanwhile, a survey of today's frantic sexual activity makes us wonder how anyone can doubt the reality of a revolution. Look at what is happening in our society:

—Underground newspapers, more neurotic than erotic, picture irreverent cartoons of prominent public leaders in various kinds of sexual escapades.

—Homosexuals, once covert but now as confident as any parading Shriner, march down city streets carrying banners which read "Gay Power" and "Gay is Good."

—Such sexploitive books as *Portnoy's Complaint* and *The Happy Hooker* make American best sellers lists in a country that only several decades ago forced the recall of a department store catalog because of its lingerie ads.

—Looking as if they just stepped off a Girl Scout cookie poster, beautiful, clean-cut girls spew four-letter Anglo-Saxon expletives at police and by-standers during political demonstrations.

—By the time they reach adolescence, today's youth are often convinced by high-pressure, low-moral advertising that the hope of success in male-female relationships rests in wearing Hai Karate or Chanel No. 5, using Ultra Brite for sexy teeth, and drinking Pepsi-Cola for perennial youth.

—Pornographic magazines, often more corn than porn, are so far out that they picture almost every kind of sexual coupling mathematically possible except, perhaps, normal heterosexual relations which are just too ordinary to sell magazines.

—Women's liberation members of such feminine organizations as SCUM (Society for Cutting Up Men) and WITCH (Woman's International Terrorist Conspiracy from Hell) campaign for the segregation of the sexes and the end of childbearing, a curiously redundant platform.

—Communes are being established throughout the country where as many as ten to twenty unrelated adults live together and have various kinds of sexual encounters, while the children of such unions wander about trying to figure out the identity of their mother, their father, and themselves.

These manifestations of sexual change are dramatic, but some serious scholars argue that there has not been a genuine revolution in sexual behavior. Catholic theologian Sidney Callahan does not believe that an actual revolution has taken place but chooses to refer to the changes as an evolution which involves a step by step advance: " 'Revolution,' in fact, seems exactly the wrong word to describe what is happening in views of sexuality; it implies a communal dash to the barricades, while sexual contact is necessarily a private, individual process of relaxation. That is, truly human sexual relations require an increase in receptivity rather than in aggressiveness." [3]

A different understanding of the current sexual scene is taken by David Mace in *The Christian Response to the Sexual Revolution*, an important book published in 1971. Mace suggests that there has indeed been a sexual revolution which has taken place in the realm of ideas. He believes that changes in ideas are leading to subsequent changes in behavior and social organization. In fact, Mace contends that the revolution in our thinking about sex is virtually over: "What we are witnessing today—a new freedom in discussing sex, in promoting it, in experimenting with it—it is not the sexual revolution, but the follow-up action that implements the revolution. The revolution itself is over, in the sense that there is now no possibility that we shall return to the ideas of the past. From now on, we shall slowly adjust our thoughts and behavior to the new concept which seems certain in time to gain almost universal acceptance." [4]

Mace thinks the change has been caused by scientific investigation, collapse of taboos, emancipation of women, medical advances, and new individual freedom. These have resulted in an open forum for discussion, a freedom to act, and a new quest for meaning.

What Mace says about the sexual revolution is correct. There has been a revolution directed against a narrow, repressive, negative, unbiblical, and unchristian view of sex which has all too frequently been a part of the teaching of the church.

The truth of the matter is that the church has too often been silent about sex, and this silence reflects a failure to meet the challenge of the sexual revolution. When the church has spoken about sex, it has frequently done so in legalistic terminology. To be sure, the picture is not entirely negative. Historical veracity demands the recollection of the fact that the church has often maintained standards of integrity and purity against a background of licentiousness and sexual anarchy. Many within the church have sought to encourage a positive approach to human sexuality. These positive ministries must continue.

Thus, the church needs to join the sexual revolution. It needs to work with those who are casting aside the negative, unbiblical view of sex that has brought guilt and misery to millions. Christians need to share in the new quest for meaning and genuine fulfillment in sexual behavior. And, the place to begin is the rethinking of the Christian understanding of sex. The barnacles of unchristian and unscientific superstition must be scraped off, so that a wholesome Christian view can appear.

What Some Women Have Said About the Sexual Revolution

How have women writers and speakers in the women's liberation movements responded to the sexual revolution? Defining the revolution in different ways, they have assessed it generally in negative terms. Obviously, many women support new openness in talking about sex and thinking about sex. They also endorse a move away from a double standard of morality. But many women see the sexual revolution as changing one kind of exploitation for another. In the pre-sexual revolution day, women were exploited sexually in the marriage relationship; now, with more sexual freedom, many women believe that they are exploited both in marriage and outside as well. Here are some ideas from women about the sexual revolution.

Speaking against the use of woman as a sex object, Betty Friedan says, "The essence of the denigration of women is their definition as sex objects, and to confront our inequality we must confront our own self-denigration and our denigration by society in these terms." She continues: "Am I saying, therefore, that women must be liberated from sex? No. I am saying that sex will only be liberated, will only cease to be a sniggering dirty joke and an obsession in this society, when women are liberated, self-determining people, liberated to a creativity beyond motherhood, to a full human creativity." [5]

Ms. Friedan warns that there is a lack of understanding in America about the enormous, buried violence of women in this country: "Like all oppressed people, women have been taking their violence out on their own bodies, in all of the maladies with which they plague the doctors' offices and the psychoanalysts. They have been taking out their violence inadvertently in subtle and insidious ways on their children and on their husbands." What Friedan wants, therefore, is a genuine revolution whereby men will be "truly liberated, to love women and to be fully themselves, when women are liberated, to be full people." [6]

Theologian Mary Daly contrasts the sexual revolution and the woman's revolution in her book *Beyond God the Father*. She calls the sexual revolution "one more extension of the politics of rape, a New Morality of false liberation foisted upon women, who have been told to be free to be what women have always been, sex objects. The difference is simply that there is now social pressure for women to be available to any male at the beckon of a once-over, to be a non-professional whore." [7]

The attack on the exploitation associated with the sexual revolution is continued by Daly: "Women's liberation is profoundly antithetical to the sexual revolution; and the second wave of feminism was energized into being largely because of the profound realization of betrayal that the 'sexual revolution' engenders." Focusing so entirely on genital sexuality is one way society rapes women by robbing them of time, energy, and self-esteem, says Daly, and she sees hope for a different kind of revolution: "The women's revolution . . . is a sexual revolution in a genuine sense of recapturing the energy that has been wrested from us by sexual politics, including the politics of the man-centered revolution." [8]

Not everyone agrees with this analysis by Ms. Daly. Such critics of women's liberation movements as Midge Decter argue that the freedom brought by the sexual revolution is one that women should embrace: "The sexual revolution which oppresses her ('the liberated woman') is a revolution made in her behalf by other women, wrested from men and assented to by them . . . in the face of the power of the revolutionaries, and not from some notion of particular advantage to themselves." [9]

The book entitled *The New Chastity and Other Arguments Against Women's Liberation* is Decter's answer to those who say that the sexual revolution has simply made it easier to exploit the female as a sex object. She argues that the women's liberation movements are not just opposed to men using women as objects; rather many in these movements are opposed to men as enemies of women. [10] Decter does not deny that the sexual revolution has failed to deliver everything that it has promised. It has failed to deliver "the promised dissolution of all erotic tension and hostility between men and women, the promised resulting happiness and completeness of women particularly." "What the new sexual freedom of women has indisputably brought them, however, is. . . new sexual freedom: the freedom of each and every individual woman to have a large hand in the determination of her own sexual conduct and destiny, the freedom to decide very largely, for herself, what to do and that other freedom, which is its inevitable concomitant, to pay very dearly—if for some reason the payment should be exacted—for her decision." [11]

Let this critic of women's liberation speak one more time: "Women's liberation is indeed nothing less than a demand on the part of those women most completely conditioned to it to repeal the sexual revolution altogether. It is a cry for the right of women to step back, retire from the disagreeable involvement in, and responsibility for, the terms of sexual equality with men." [12]

One women's liberation spokesman who has moved from new left causes to radical feminism is Robin Morgan. She believes that the sexual revolution has exploited women: "Good bye to the Hip Culture and to the so-called Sexual Revolution, which has functioned toward women's freedom as did the Reconstruction toward former slaves—reinstituted oppression by another name." [13]

Theologian Rosemary Ruether has discussed what she calls the "Puritan-Prurient" syndrome, by which she means that sex is either repressed in an ascetic sort of way or sex is used to depersonalize woman in a libertine manner. She says that "today people are seeking to throw off the long heritage of sexual repression. But what the media call the 'sexual revolution' often does little more than establish the prurient side of this puritan schism." [14]

Dr. Ruether says that the sexual revolution came at just the right time in our society which was being transformed from a capitalistic society to a hedonistic culture of consumers. This kind of society calls on a domesticated woman's sexual image to whet the appetite for wasteful consumption. Thus, the sexual revolution which was initiated to help women reclaim their right to sexual experience deteriorated into a movement which simply oppressed women as objects: "In the popular culture, sexual frankness begins to look more and more like pornography and carries increasingly sadistic overtones. In patriarchal cultures, the two sides of the same psycho-social alienation are still manifest in the repression and exploitation of women as both the despised and the desired-body object. In all these contexts, it is not the liberation of women that surfaces but the prurient side of puritan repression." [15]

One by-product of the sexual revolution is a great increase in the amount of pornography in our society. Because pornography does special damage to the personhood of women, it deserves careful attention here.

Women and Pornography

One of the most blatant and dehumanizing forms of discrimination against women is pornography. It is made by men for men, but the result is exploitation of women. (Even the magazines like *Viva* and *Playgirl* may be for men, according to some experts who think that these are really homosexual magazines. In any case, most pornography is by men for men.)

What we are talking about here is not the subtle obscenities that women face every day—the idea that woman is a defective male, the view that she is inferior to man. What we are dealing with is that explicit pornography which uses women, or more precisely their bodies, to satisfy the lustful fantasies of men. Women's liberation movements should launch a campaign against obscenity. From time to time we do hear about a demonstration against Hugh Hefner or some other figure associated with sexual exploitation. But what is needed is a major movement to try to control this unwholesome exploitation of women. The truth of the matter is that pornography is male chauvinism incarnate.

The problem with pornography is not that it tells too much about women but that it tells too little. It claims to reveal all when in reality it practices a kind of censorship by turning women into bodies and by neglecting the fact that they are really human beings.

Fortunately, Christianity is a corrective to the pornography faced by our society. Here is a comparison of pornography and a Christian view of sex which can be used to combat this form of discrimination against women.

1. In pornography sex is limited almost entirely to its physical dimension; a Christian view understands sex as an aspect of personhood which permeates our total being. Always promising to tell everything about sex, pornographers tell us very little about what sex really is. Contrast its mechanical view with the multidimensional view of sex in the best of Christian thought.

2. Pornography advocates no controls on sexual expression, thus sowing seeds for moral anarchy; in a Christian view, the power of sex is recognized, and responsible controls are called for. Unlike pornography, the Bible recognizes the dynamite of sex and offers guidance for responsible stewardship of this gift of God.

3. In pornography sex is associated with destructive, sick humor; a Christian view links sex with wholesome joy and laughter. Pornography knows nothing of the kind of happy celebration of sex found in the Song of Solomon.

4. In pornography sex is tied to a fantasy world; a Christian view prepares one to see sex as a part of the real world created by God. Pornography provides props for those who want to escape from reality to a dream world. But these dreams soon become nightmares! Christianity gives one the moral resources to choose to work with God to enjoy the real world as he intended.

5. Pornography presents an inaccurate comprehension of the male and female; a Christian view offers an understanding of the male and female as God's creatures. Pornography tries to

make us believe that a male and a female are the sum of their private parts. It pictures man as a super-sexual being. The woman is seen as a toy, and, if she gets broken or destroyed, as toys usually do, she can be replaced. In a Christian view, the male and female have dignity and worth because they are God's creatures.

6. Pornography really portrays not relationships but the proximity of bodies; a Christian view calls for a covenant relationship in which a married couple can share the totality of life's experiences from giving birth to facing death.

7. Pornography often links sex to perversion, pain, torture, and sadism. In a Christian view, sex is related to wholesome pleasure. While pornography often uses sex as an expression of hostility, the Bible points to the good of sharing and meeting the sexual needs of one's mate (Eph. 5:22-33).

8. Pornography ignores the mystery of sex; a Christian view recognizes that sex cannot be fully appreciated apart from its mystery. Pornography misses the element of mystery and wonder in "the way of a man with a maid" (Prov. 30:19).

Though pornography claims to tell it like it is, it dangerously distorts the truth. It is deceitful about sexuality, which is one of the most important aspects of our lives. Because its distortions can mislead us and rob us of pleasure and truth, we have a responsibility to tell it like it is about pornography.

Although it is not legally obscene, one particularly serious form of discrimination against women is the portrayal of women in contemporary advertising; whereas pornography is usually sold in adult stores or passed through the mail, the abuse of women through advertising is seen by all of us every day. Such exploitive advertising is dehumanizing. Women are pictured as objects. They are used as a means to sell products. They are treated not as full-dimensional human beings but as one-dimensional bodies.

Today, for example, all ages hear that Ultra Brite tooth paste is good not only for cleaning teeth but also for giving "sex appeal." One learns that Howard Clothes makes clothes "for men who make babies." A young man who wants to score a success with his girl is advised by her: "Move up to Chrysler, Marty. We'll make it easy." The makers of Intimate perfume get their point across by asking: "What makes a shy girl get Intimate?" And, the makers of Noxzema Medicated Shave Cream have turned a ordinary product into an aphrodisiac by associating it with a blond who sang: "Take it off! Take it all off!"

The list of exploitative advertising slogans is endless. But the truth of the matter is that such advertising seems to work in our society. This raises a question about what kind of economic system we have that has to depend upon the exploitation of women in particular and sex in general in order to sell us products.

What the Sexual Revolution Means for Women

To conclude this discussion of women and the sexual revolution, take a look at some theses about the meaning of this revolution for women. Many of the implications that will be offered here are for men as well.

In discussing the sexual revolution, we will continue to follow the view that the sexual revolution is a change in ideas, a revolutionary change in our thinking about sex, which has already taken place and which is bringing about subsequent changes in behavior.

1. The double standard of sexual behavior will continue to diminish in our society. It is probable that the double standard grew out of the belief that women are the property of men. Although the property view has largely disappeared in the American culture, the double standard has continued. No doubt some will continue to maintain this double standard, but for an increasing number of people the double standard is being replaced by a single standard of greater sexual permissiveness.

The demise of the double standard (but not the increase in sexual permissiveness) is desirable for several reasons. It is hypocritical and ethically inconsistent for a man to demand sexual freedom for himself but sexual integrity for his partner. The discriminatory attitude of the double standard is decidedly inferior to a standard of mutuality between the sexes.

The double standard attitude also hinders sexual adjustment within marriage. The male who practices the double standard has sexual experience with women he does not respect almost solely for the purpose of self-satisfaction, and he develops feelings of disgust toward such women. This will hamper adjustment between a husband and his wife also.

The double standard creates two classes of women: the "good" and the "bad." This leads to exploitation of those women of lower economic classes and to the use of such persons as mere things. Such an attitude, therefore, is inconsistent with the Christian understanding of personhood.

2. Everybody singing the praises of the sexual revolution is not for true freedom. Many men and some women support a sexual revolution, not to have better ideas and attitudes about sex but simply to have more opportunities for sexual exploitation. This is a reality which women and men dare not ignore.

The sexual revolution is a convenient aphrodisiac used to move many people into sexual experiences for which they are unready and unprepared. The sexual revolution coerces some to conform to unwanted sexual life-styles. "Thou shalt not" has been replaced by "Thou shalt" in many circles, and the effects on personal integrity and emotional stability have often been devastating.

There will always be men who want to coerce women into sexual affairs, and there are an increasing number of women who want to do the same to men. For such people the sexual revolution is a convenient rationale.

3. A better scientific understanding of sex can aid people in their sexual expression. No doubt there is much nonsense being offered as sexual therapy in our society. Nevertheless, real gains have been made which can lead to more healthy sexual understanding and expression.

What has science taught us? From the field of physiology,

for example, come the reports of Masters and Johnson entitled *Human Sexual Response* and *Human Sexual Inadequacy.* In their first report Masters and Johnson dealt with: (1) investigations in conceptive physiology (with clinical application in the treatment of conceptive inadequacy); (2) research in contraceptive physiology (with clinical orientation to problems of population control); and (3) definition of sexual physiology (with clinical focus on the causes and treatment of human sexual inadequacy). In their second major report, *Human Sexual Inadequacy,* the authors indicate how knowledge about sexual functioning can be used to help men and women overcome sexual difficulties.

One who doubts the importance of physiology and biology for a Christian interpretation of sex need only recall that Aquinas thought that man's response during orgasm was due to a lack of reason which came with the Fall in the Garden of Eden. Aquinas and his fellow churchmen did not understand the neural mechanism which caused orgasm. As D. S. Bailey points out:

they were unaware that the phenomena which they attributed to the effect of the Fall were actually ordained by God as a part of the normal operation of the human body; and the coitus in Paradise, as they conceived it, was not only unnatural but also impossible. Thus advances in scientific knowledge have rendered untenable a view of physical sexuality which has obsessed the mind of the Church for more than 15 centuries, and has profoundly and adversely influenced the sexual attitudes of the West.[16]

Scientific insight has also corrected the superstitious reverence for the male semen and the accompanying belief that the woman was only an incubator to provide a place in which the semen could produce a child. This view, now disproved by the discovery of ovulation, contributed to the subordination of woman even in Christian circles.

At the same time, Christians must reject those pseudo-scientists who use the guise of science to provide erotic exploitation.

For example, a movie entitled *Man and Woman* was recently shown in Nashville at a so-called adult theater. From the newspaper ads, it appears that this is pseudo-scientific pornography. It claims to be a "visual marriage manual in color" which will teach "49 ways [translate positions] revealing a new world waiting to be explored by husbands and wives who really love each other!"

While Christians must be willing to listen and to study the valuable information available in the findings of modern sciences, it must also be recognized that science is limited in its treatment of sexuality. Excessive dependence upon science can lead to a laboratory approach to sex in which the element of mystery is neglected or ignored. The Bible teaches that there is wonder in "the way of a man with a maid." This is a quality that cannot be measured by electrodes or plotted on charts.

Failure to understand the limitations of science has led to the *marriage manual fallacy.* Most of these manuals stress the competence of performance. Their intention is to cultivate sexual athletes who will be able to perform properly. The reward they offer is a utopia of sexual pleasure. To be sure, some manuals can be useful. However, many more fall into the fallacy of separating performance from a covenant of mutuality. And the boasts of some manuals are utterly absurd! For example, a brochure for one sensational manual promises: "We guarantee that in less than seven days this amazing book will make you a SEXUAL SUPERMAN and turn you into one of the world's truly great lovers."

Sexual gymnastics will not produce sexual supermen and women in seven days or seven lifetimes! As Rollo May points out in *Love and Will:*

it often occurs to me that there is an inverse relationship between the number of how-to-do-it books perused by a person or rolling off the presses in a society and the amount of sexual passion or even pleasure experienced by the persons involved. Certainly nothing is wrong with technique as such, in playing golf or acting or making love. But the emphasis beyond a certain point on technique and sex makes for a mechanistic attitude toward love-making, and goes along with alienation, feelings of loneliness, and depersonalization.[17]

Science can help us but it must be joined with the insights of Christian theology.

4. The increasing separation of sex and reproduction in our society will continue. In light of the population explosion which is threatening the world with famine, disease, and war, this aspect of the sexual revolution needs to be explored. On the one hand, the best of Christian thought has linked sex and reproduction. (For that matter, some of the worst in Christian thought has done the same thing!) Christianity has taught that sexual intercourse belongs in a covenant that shares a totality of life including the possibility of reproduction. On the other hand, there is a worldwide population explosion which we cannot ignore. Population must be controlled. But we must also resist those who say that sex and reproduction do not have to be joined at all.

Physical and other factors sometimes make pregnancy impossible or unwise for a couple. But usually, having a child is a natural outgrowth of a covenant in which a couple share all life's experiences. Having too many children is unwise. Voluntarily having no children is usually unwise also.

5. Women (and men) will increasingly have greater liberty for sexual experimentation. The mobility of the contemporary American society makes this liberty readily available. The anonymity of an urban culture assures that one can usually act without being seen. There is no evidence that sexual experimentation will leave the American scene anytime soon.

The practice of having sexual intercourse outside of marriage will continue. There is evidence that premarital sexual intercourse is taking place more frequently among some economic classes in our society now than it has in the past. This trend will continue, as will the frequency of sexual intercourse by married people outside the covenant of marriage. Christians can back up a condemnation of such practices with careful explanations of why these practices are wrong from a Christian point of view.

6. There is a new climate in our society which makes it possible to do something about discrimination based on gender. The consciousness of the American people is slowly being raised. The exploitation of women goes unnoticed less frequently. Perhaps some communities have not gotten the message yet, but the powerful influence of the media is changing that. The sexual revolution will lead eventually to less discrimination against women.

As an outgrowth of the struggle by women to be free, hostility between the sexes will increase in our society. As women seek to change roles and gain rights, many men will resist. Eventually there will be a more healthy interaction between the sexes as men and women meet each other as equals. This is not to say that we are moving toward a utopia of sexual rights. But the situation will improve.

The Christian churches in America will be a source of some opposition to women who seek emancipation, but they will be a source of greater help. Obviously a culture of chauvinist discrimination has crept into the churches. But there are also present the resources in the Christian faith for eliminating discrimination against women. Churches are not unified in this matter, and there will be skirmishes; but the ultimate result will be assistance in the Christian community for the freedom of women.

The sexual revolution opens the door to more wholesome sexual expression for women and men. But it may also lead to greater exploitation and oppression. Each individual must decide which door to enter. Christians can offer the good news about sex which will lead to fulfillment and integrity. Through Jesus Christ there can be not only temporary liberation, but a lifetime of genuine freedom.

Notes

1. Betty Friedan, "Our Revolution Is Unique," *Voices of the New Feminism,* edited by Mary Lu Thompson (Boston: Beacon Press, 1970), p. 37.

2. Vancouver Study Group, "Polarity of Men and Women," *The Biblical and Theological Understanding of Sexuality and Family Life,* report of a Study of the Faith and Order Commission of the Canadian Council of Churches, November, 1969, p. 30.

3. Sidney Callahan, "Human Sexuality in a Time of Change," *The Christian Century* (Aug. 28, 1968), p. 1077.

4. David Mace, *The Christian Response to the Sexual Revolution* (Nashville: Abingdon Press, 1970).

5. Friedan, *op. cit.,* p. 35.

6. *Ibid.,* p. 36.

7. Mary Daly, *Beyond God the Father* (Boston: Beacon Press, 1973), p. 122.

8. *Ibid.,* pp. 122-24.

9. Midge Decter, "The Liberated Women," quoted by Judith Hole and Ellen Levine in *Rebirth of Feminism* (New York: Quadrangle Books, 1971), p. 218.

10. Decter, *The New Chastity and Other Arguments Against Women's Liberation* (New York: Coward, McCann, and Geoghegan, Inc., 1972), pp. 95 ff.

11. *Ibid.,* pp. 94-95.

12. *Ibid.*

13. Robin Morgan, "Good Bye to All That" in Roszak and Roszak, *op. cit.,* p. 243.

14. Rosemary Radford Ruether, "Sexism in the Theology of Liberation and the Theology of Liberation," *The Christian Century* (Dec. 12, 1973), p. 1225.

15. *Ibid.,* pp. 1225-26.

16. Derrick Sherwin Bailey, *Sexual Relation in Christian Thought* (New York: Harper and Brothers, 1959), p. 245.

17. Rollo May, *Love and Will* (New York: Wm. Norton & Company, 1965), p. 43.

11

A Christian Approach to Women and Health

Sarah Frances Anders

The concept of "good health" is a comprehensive one including social, physical, mental, and spiritual well-being. It is more than the absence of illness; it is a positive attitude toward life and a cheerful acceptance of the responsibilities and relationships of living. How much of good health is due to heredity and how much to environment (including culture) is still a moot issue. There are some propensities for certain defects and diseases that are assumed to be prenatal, if not inherited, such as diabetes, particular bone deficiencies, and perhaps even some allergic conditions. Some mental disorders are traceable to biochemical abnormalities, brain tumors, and now even to the presence of an extra sex chromosome.

Just as individuals are unique with respect to predispositions to health conditions, there are also sex-related health factors. Medical scientists have known for some decades that women enjoy considerable protection against heart disease for the first forty years or so of their lives. The female hormone diminishes the accumulation of cholesterol and fatty acids in the inner lining of the arteries that would make one prone to heart attacks. Physical defects or inherited traits that may handicap full social performance among males include conditions such as hemophilia and color blindness.

The relationship between mood and physical conditions would warrant a dissertation in itself! The Greeks, centuries before the time of Christ, pondered the inextricable relations between the *psyche* and the *soma;* the concept of psychosomatic disorders is almost a contemporary household phrase! It appears that the hormonal cycles of women, in which there are varying levels of estrogen and progesterone, may be associated with mood changes although there is considerable individual variation. Just before menstruation, during menopause, and immediately following childbirth, there may be tendencies to experience more depression, fatigue, anxiety, or other negative emotions.[1] Recently, research has suggested the possibility that men may also have hormone cycles of approximately thirty days, with accompanying psychic changes. Whether further research corroborates this or not, the fact remains that levels of testosterone certainly vary among men and there is an important behavioral correlate there.[2] How much mood variation is biologically induced and how much is due to generations of conditioning that make women *expect* to be moody at certain cyclical periods (a surprising number of women claim to be creative and energetic at these same times!) and that many men assume their emotions will plateau to a greater extent or will reflect personality rather than biological variations—these relationships are difficult to determine.

The State of Women

When one examines behavioral statistics of women during the early 1970's, it seems that women continue to be more durable, although not stronger and bigger. Mortality rates alone would support the durability of the female, since her life expectancy is at least half a decade longer than a male's—into the mid-seventies. As will be pointed out, new life-styles for men and women could diminish this difference. Since prehistoric times, both sexes have grown taller and more durable, but the differences in size and other health factors may disappear as their roles overlap more and more.

This increasing similarity of health behavior is apparent in the number of days persons are restricted from their normal routines. Women have only about two more restrictive days (16+ vs. 14+) than men per year and this difference is probably still related to pregnancy and childbirth, as well as the fact that half of the women do not have the pressure to "be at work." As the birthrate has declined, the differences in restricted days has also declined. Interesting differences still occur in the causes for restriction: women are more apt to have bed restriction and both chronic or acute reasons, whereas men are more likely to have injuries. Work loss, however, is very weakly associated with sex; age and class differences are much more related to absence from work.[3]

At least four causes of death are increasing for both men and women—cardiovascular illnesses, malignancy, vehicular accidents, and suicides (a slight increase); but among these, malignancy is higher for women than men. The causes of death which have declined significantly have been influenza and pneumonia, tuberculosis, syphilis, and diabetes; the rates for all of these are about the same for the two sexes, except diabetes which is still a greater killer of women.

The most encouraging mortality statistic for women could be the plummeting maternal death rate, now accounting for only one out of two hundred thousand deaths. Toxemia (accounting for about one third of all maternal deaths) and complications following childbirth or abortion are the major problems; but nonwhites have a rate four times higher than white women.

There are decided sex differentials with respect to lung cancer, ulcers, and cirrhosis of the liver, in favor of women. Somewhat fewer women smoke than men (31 percent compared to 47 percent of the men) and women smoke less often; so, this may be the major factor in the lower incidence of lung cancer among females. Ulcers are reported for only one third as many women patients as men, but should women join the ranks of management and competitive professions to a greater degree this could possibly change. Only good "guesstimates" are available on the actual number of alcoholics in American (probably between nine and a half to eleven million); but since most studies show that men outnumber women about three to one in problem drinking, it is not surprising that cirrhosis of the liver still predominates among men.

As previously mentioned, women are not as accident-prone

as men with respect to vehicular use. Men had about three times as many fatal accidents as women throughout the 1960's, and death potential paralleled the average miles driven per capita during a year. Men were also more apt to be killed as pedestrians. Should women enter traveling vocations to any great extent rather than just going to and from home, a change might be expected in these statistics.

Women have also had more favorable homicide and suicide rates for years and there are interesting observations to be made at this point. Though women kill and are victims of homicide less often, they are nonetheless involved in 54 percent of the spouse/spouse homicides and 51 percent of those involving lovers. Romantic and family situations are more apt to prompt women to kill or be killed. For a long time they were more apt to make suicide "attempts" than to succeed at this pattern of death. These were interpreted as bids for attention and cries for help or affection. Now there are definite indications that female suicide is on the rise, in some cities such as Los Angeles reaching as high as 45 percent of all cases; but the reasons associated with these deaths are different from, and hazier than, those of men.[4] Since suicides among females peak between the ages of forty-five and fifty-four, the middle-years syndrome of "empty nest" frustrations, unfulfilling work situations, and marital tensions appears to be a plausible explanation. There has always been the possibility that many "accidental" deaths among women could have been suicides, if the broader situational factors were considered.

Chronic Health Problems Among Women

From the Christian perspective, there are some recurring health problems of women that may have moral and ethical implications for current patterns of living. Hypertension is a growing concern for all Americans, but recent studies indicate that women account for 60 percent of all patients with high blood pressure and 50 percent of the two hundred thousand deaths annually which are due to strokes.[5] The use of the birth control pill might account for a small portion of these cases of high blood pressure and the surgical removal of estrogen-producing ovaries would also be a factor. Estimates differ widely concerning the number of needless hysterectomies. One study indicated that less than one third of such operations were medically justified (women's liberationists have called the other hysterectomies "remunerectomies").[6] Others have estimated 20 percent were unjustified and cited researchers such as Dr. John Bunker of Stanford University, who stated that American surgeons perform about three hundred more hysterectomies per hundred thousand population than English or Welsh doctors.[7]

But hypertension is obviously related to the fact that women seem to be experiencing more conflict in today's society. A University of Wisconsin study indicated that women patients today complain of greater anxiety, depression, alienation, and inability to cope with stress than such patients did a decade ago. No such trend seemed to be present among men.[8] While anxiety can be related to high blood pressure, it is also apparent that women in our culture may be permitted to complain more about their anxieties (this could be a safety valve), whereas men may bottle them up and then break down more completely in their mental and physical health.

Another indication in the current behavioral patterns of American women is overmedication, a situation due in part to doctors overwhelmed by the promises made by pharmaceutical advertising and in part to self-treatment. More than one report has indicated that as many as forty-five million women have been on tranquilizers. Encouraged by drug company claims, perhaps many doctors overreact to symptoms of the normal routine anxieties of daily life and prescribe powerful pills. As many as two out of three women have been using such drugs, presumably prescribed by their doctors.[9]

It is difficult to ascertain just how many women move on to addiction, whether from experimentation with marijuana and hard drugs or from prescription use. Estimates of women drug addicts vary between 15 and 20 percent of the total known addicts.[10] Whether women are seeking in drugs what they once found in prayer, church activities, or their vicarious involvement in their children's and husbands' lives remains an unanswered question. Nevertheless, the church should provide one of the avenues for understanding anxiety, frustrations, and need for such dependencies. The enlistment of women particularly during their middle years in meaningful church ministries could be a partial approach to the problems they experience, as well as a boon to most church programs.

After heart disease and cancer, the biggest health problem in America may well be alcoholism; it certainly is the greatest part of the drug problem. Most deaths from cirrhosis of the liver (thirteen thousand per year), as previously suggested, are related to alcoholism and there is no doubt that this addiction shortens life by ten to twenty years. The National Mental Health Institute recently pointed out the increase in female alcoholics, one for every three men with the problem. This is a minimum estimate, for the nonworking woman can hide her habit more easily. Women still begin to drink heavily at a later age than men, but they deteriorate into alcoholism more rapidly. The fact that drinking is a more accepted social pattern for both sexes is indicated by the 26 percent increase in the per capita consumption of alcoholic beverages during the 1960's. Test results have been contradictory as to whether men or women are more taste-prone to alcohol, but there is the possibility that the lesser weight and size of the woman moves her more quickly to drunkenness and problem drinking.[11]

The church has often directed its attention toward the problems of alcohol in a condemning rather than an educational, counseling, and rehabilitative manner. Frequently it has been stressed more in youth education, but the roots of the problems of drugs and alcohol in the youth culture lie in the accepted martini-sipping, pill-taking behavior of an adult culture which may include a considerable sprinkling of church members. Adults equally need the Christian perspective of such an educational thrust, for they confront it daily in a world that accepts it casually and that tends to treat the nondrinker as the deviant. While not respective of sex particularly, obesity may be second only to alcoholism and drug abuse in its epidemic and moral implications for Americans. Whether overweight is due to glandular disturbances or emotional frustration, the dangers to mental and physical health are the same. In a world in which over two billion people are undernourished, the suicidal potential of overeating seems blatantly immoral. What about the moral implications of an advertising climate, especially in women's magazines, in which food products and rich gourmet meals are promoted by voguishly slim females who obviously have not partaken! Aside from vanity appeals, the threat to heart disease, back, and kidney ailments is a well-known fact. Overweight women have a 61 percent higher death rate than same age women of normal weight.[12] Perhaps some churches that have included weight-watching and exercise classes in their activities programs are contributing as much to the moral and mental health of their members as through any other so-called religious programs!

Taking Care of Self

Sociologist Ruth Cavan has defined suicide as more than the act of taking one's own life; she has seen it as the conscious or unconscious refusal to protect oneself from destruction. The desire for good health and self-preservation is more than a basic law of life or good logic; it is also for the Christian the natural extension of the commandment "Love thyself," implied in the second law, "Love thy neighbor as thyself." (As an aside, many in church-related vocations and dedicated laypersons practice poor stewardship of "self" and even a kind of spiritual suicide when they deny good care of self in the pursuit of "service to God and mankind.") Any Christian approach to health care, then, must encompass preventive, as well as curative and rehabilitative, measures for healthy attitudes and physical functioning. Thus it is for women as well as all persons!

Women who seek good insight into their unique health problems and into the best care of themselves discover that the American medical field is male-dominated. Women make up the largest segment of the population going to doctors (25 percent more visits per year), taking more prescription drugs (50 percent more than men), and going to the hospital. Yet, over 90 percent of the doctors are men and they dominate a field of health services in which 70 percent are women workers. There are proportionately fewer women doctors in only three other countries—South Vietnam, Madagascar, and Spain.[13]

Second only to a positive attitude about self-care is a good doctor-patient relationship, and this is far more difficult for many to achieve. In this day of harried, overworked physicians, it is not always easy to locate either general practitioners or gynecologists/obstetricians in whom you not only have utmost confidence with respect to professional competence but who possess special empathy with the female psyche and with Christian value systems. The doctor who not only can direct you to nontechnical literature on such common female problems as vaginitis, endometriosis, cervical erosion, cystitis, breast and cervical cancer, but who can also listen and counsel sympathetically when even an educated woman asks naive, illformed questions about herself may still be found; but such credentials are not given in the local medical directory! One of the best guides to finding a doctor is given in *Our Bodies Our Selves,* but it does not provide the insights just mentioned either.[14]

The third call is for Christian activism when good health is jeopardized by establishment practices. Adequate preventive and protective legislation has almost been accomplished in the areas of work-hours and safety measures. But thinking Christians need to be aware of, and aggressive in the elimination of, such hazards as too slow enforcement of Federal Drug Administration rulings on harmful or ineffective drugs. Studies, as long as five to ten years ago, on the hazards of diet pills, vaginal deodorants, and certain cosmetics have not been enough to get them removed from the market because they represent millions, even billions, of dollars to their respective companies.

After 369 drugs had been rated hazardous by the FDA two and one-half years earlier, 200 of them were still on the market in 1970—and many persons considered them "good" drugs because they had been prescribed by their doctors. How many "Christian" doctors can keep up enough with their field to inform their patients that 29,000 people died in 1970 from "good" drugs? Since women probably account for 80 percent of the diet-pill users and 76 percent of the tranquilizer users, they are the logical pressure group for better education and restrictions from the government.[15]

The beginning point to good health is the ending as well. Women (persons) should appreciate their bodies and minds, recognize their uniqueness, and set aside prudishness or false modesty in pursuing good health. The spiritual self is an integral part of successful searching for good health.

Notes

1. For a fuller discussion, cf. Judith Bardwick, *Psychology of Women: A Study of Bio-Cultural Conflicts* (New York: Harper & Row, 1971), pp. 28-29.

2. Estelle Ramey, "Men's Cycles," *Ms.* (Spring, 1972), pp. 8-14.

3. These and subsequent "State of Women" statistics are supported by Abbott L. Ferris, *Indicators of Trends in the Status of American Women* (Russell Sage Fdn., 1971).

4. "Situation Report (Behavior)," *Time* 99, No. 12 (March 20, 1972), p. 47.

5. Ralph Bugg, "Husband, Take Care of Her Heart," *Today's Health* 47 (November, 1969), pp. 52-55.

6. Paul Lembke, "Medical Auditing," cited in *Our Bodies Our Selves* (The Boston Women's Health Book Collective, Inc., 1971, 1973), p. 238.

7. "How Gynecologists Can Fulfill the Intimate Needs of Today's Woman," *Today's Health* 51 (May, 1973), pp. 20-21.

8. *Time, op. cit.*

9. Roland H. Bert, "The Overmedicated Woman," *McCall's* 98 (September, 1971), p. 67.

10. *Time, op. cit.;* and Bernard Barber in *Drugs For and Against* (New York: Hart Publishing Co., Inc., 1970).

11. "Alcoholism: New Victims, New Treatments," *Time* 103 (April 22, 1974), pp. 75-81.

12. Gary Null, *Body Pollution* (New York: Arco, 1973), p. 17.

13. *Our Bodies Our Selves, op. cit.*, p. 237.

14. *Ibid.*, pp. 244 ff.

15. Ellen Frankfort, *Vaginal Politics* (Bantam Books, 1972), Chapter 11, pp. 96 ff.

12

A Christian Understanding of Abortion

David Mace

Sally Brown was decidedly nervous when she arrived at the clinic. She didn't quite know what was going to happen. Her appointment was for nine o'clock, and that was only ten minutes away. She reminded herself that she had made her decision, and there was no turning back now. Then she took a deep breath and walked right in.

She found herself in a large waiting room with four or five other women, sitting around in comfortable chairs. Sally went up to the reception desk and gave her name. "Please take a seat," said the receptionist. "We'll call you when we're ready."

About half an hour later her first name was called. She was taken to a room where she filled out a personal form, and a nurse asked her some questions about her medical history. When this was finished, she went to the cashier's office and paid the clinic fee.

After some lab tests, she joined a group counseling session. The counselor explained to the group of women that they would have their abortions done by the D and E method because they all had early pregnancies. The method was explained in detail, and they were encouraged to ask questions. The counselor answered the questions courteously and invited the women to talk about how they felt. One girl seemed quite upset and the counselor asked her to stay behind so she could talk with her alone.

Sally was now shown a cubicle where she undressed and put on a hospital gown. When she was ready, she was taken to the operating room, where she met the physician. The nurse then placed her on the table in the usual position for a pelvic examination. The doctor gave her a local anesthetic, her cervix was dilated, and a plastic tube, half an inch in diameter, was inserted in her uterus. When everything was ready, the suction pump connected to the tube was switched on for a few minutes. Sally felt a little discomfort, but no pain. The physician checked to see that the contents of the uterus had been emptied into the waiting jar, then covered it up. A few minutes later, Sally was helped to get down from the table, and taken to the recovery room.

She stayed there for an hour and a half. During this time a nurse monitored her pulse, her breathing, her blood pressure, her temperature, and her heartbeat. She was asked to report if she felt any severe cramps, and a watch was kept for any signs of heavy bleeding.

The nurse asked Sally how she felt. She confessed she had been a little dizzy at first, but maybe this was because she had not been allowed to eat any food that day. She said she was all right now. The nurse said she could get up and walk about a little. She was given some light refreshments.

By this time she was feeling herself again. She noticed that it was 2:30 in the afternoon. The nurse gave her a final check and took her back to the cubicle where she had left her clothes. She dressed, and half an hour later she was on her way home again. It was all over.

What I have described is a typical abortion, carried out in the first three months of pregnancy, without complications. This is now happening, with full legal approval, all over the United States, to about two women every minute.

For each of these women, a personal problem is being solved. And in each case, the mutilated remains of a beginning human life are left behind in a jar.

How are we to react to this? What does it all mean? How should we interpret it—theologically, socially, ethically?

A Brief Historical Summary

First, let's see how it all came about.

We are living in the wake of the sexual revolution. After long centuries of negative repression, we have discovered the goodness of sex. As a result, we are enjoying sex as never before. And we are having problem pregnancies as never before.

In a sense, the sexual revolution has itself been the result of a problem pregnancy. It was born just a little prematurely. Two generations of young people have now been assured that they could enjoy sexual freedom, because the perfect contraceptive was just around the corner. At the same time, married people have been told about the perils of the population explosion, and encouraged to enjoy their sex lives but to limit their families. Contraceptives, they were assured, could enable them to do this.

Unfortunately, the perfect contraceptive is still around the corner and even the imperfect ones we have are sometimes out of reach. Technology has achieved great marvels, but it has still failed to deliver on its promise in this area. The result is a steadily increasing frequency of problem pregnancies, producing a trail of human misery. Finally, in desperation, we have been compelled to provide legal abortion as a second line of defense to deal with the resulting crisis.

All this has come upon us with startling suddenness. Only a few years ago, abortion was something people—nice people—didn't talk about. It was something dark and sinister. It was a criminal act, contrary to the law. Most doctors were strongly against it. As recently as 1967, the American Medical Association adopted a stated policy of opposition to induced abortion, except where the health or life of the mother was threatened, or under other extreme and exceptional conditions. The churches, until very recently, regarded abortion with horror.

Then, almost overnight, the entire climate changed. Never in the history of social ethics, I believe, has any culture made such a dramatic about-face on an ethical question of such vital importance. Pressure groups sprang up everywhere. Members of the Women's Liberation Movement, divided into factions about almost everything else, found that the liberalizing of abortion was the one issue on which they could all agree. The youth culture, led by activist student groups, campaigned vigorously for free abortion. The population control movement saw it as a way to cut back sharply on the birthrate. Under these pressures, state laws began to be changed. By 1970 doctors were deeply divided, and soon they were changing their minds in droves. Clergymen joined in and organized services to help women to get abortions. Churches began to pass resolutions in support of liberalization of the law. As the mind-changing process gathered momentum, the Catholics tried desperately to organize the opposition; but the extreme position they took prevented moderates from joining them. By 1971, in a plebiscite taken in the State of Washington, a liberalization law was voted in by a small minority.

By this time the bandwagon was really rolling. Delighted by the rapidity of their success, the abortion campaigners stepped up their demands. Liberal laws were no longer enough. Abortion freely available on request became the declared objective. So now, in states that passed liberal laws, the ink was hardly dry before the campaign started all over again, this time for repeal of all abortion laws.

Meanwhile, appeals to the Supreme Court were piling up, and an early verdict was promised. The furor died down, except for some increased vigor in the Catholic campaign. The pro-abortion campaigners had played their ace, and they waited for the final verdict of the supreme legal authority.

That verdict, as we all know, was announced early in 1973. The Supreme Court, with seven justices in favor and two opposed, struck down most of the abortion laws in the country and opened the gate wide for abortion on request. The matter was thus apparently settled for a long time to come.

I have skimmed very lightly over the crowded events of the past seven years and left out a great deal. But I hope I have conveyed a sense of the break-neck pace at which we have moved. Many people have been bewildered and almost stunned by it all. In a few short years entrenched traditional attitudes have been attacked, overwhelmed, and swept away. There can be no doubt about it, the supporters of liberal abortion have won a tremendous victory. The stunned and shocked statements of Catholic bishops, commenting on the Supreme Court decision, testified eloquently to this fact.

The Supreme Court Decision

Let's take a closer look at the judgment of the Supreme Court. It's a very interesting document. Most people know about it; but I expect few have had time to go through the entire original document. So, let me try to summarize it.

The Court chose to base its ruling on two particular appeals. Both came from southern states—one from Texas, the other from Georgia. The main judgment was based on the Texas case, and I'll confine my comments to that one.

A pregnant, single woman challenged the Texas abortion law, which wouldn't allow her an abortion because her life was not threatened by the pregnancy. She couldn't afford to travel to another state. She claimed that the Texas law abridged her right to privacy and claimed that it should therefore be ruled unconstitutional.

Before coming to a decision, the Court made a careful survey of the history of abortion. In effect, this survey led to two broad general conclusions.

First, the Court decided that there has been a tendency in our culture to interpret legal attitudes on abortion in the past too rigidly. For example, it now appears doubtful whether in English common law abortion was ever really regarded as a serious crime. Since it was from English common law that the early American laws were derived, obviously the legislators over here had a bias and gave their laws a decidedly puritanical twist. So it was argued that if we now pass more liberal laws, we are not departing from our ancient tradition but rather returning to it.

Second, the Court decided that changing conditions today have undermined the main reasons for which the original state laws were passed. A major state interest is the health of the woman. In the old days, abortion was very dangerous, and women had to be protected from that danger. Nowadays, the situation is reversed, because abortions up to twelve weeks actually involve less risk to the woman than she would face if she gave birth to the child. So, the ground is cut away from the argument behind most abortion laws, that their purpose is to protect the woman's health and life.

For lawmakers, these are both powerful arguments. It is clear that they weighed heavily with the Supreme Court. In addition, the plea of the Texas woman that her privacy had been abridged was accepted, although the Court did *not* accept the position of the Women's Liberation Movement that the right of personal privacy is absolute. The judges declared that this right is always qualified and conditional.

So far, I haven't mentioned the rights of the unborn. Some commentators think the Supreme Court ducked the issue. You have probably read the much-quoted statement: "We need not resolve the difficult question of where life begins. When those trained in the respective disciplines of medicine, philosophy, and theology are unable to arrive at any consensus, the judiciary, at this point in the development of man's knowledge, is not in a position to speculate as to the answer."

In fact, the justices *don't* really duck this question. They examine it, rather convincingly, from their own legal point of view; and interestingly enough, they quote religious practice to support their position. Listen to this: "Life takes time to develop, and until it is actually present, it cannot be destroyed. Its interruption prior to formation would hardly be homicide, and society does not regard it as such. The rites of Baptism are not performed and death certificates (and funerals, we might add) are not required when a miscarriage occurs—this would be the case if the fetus constituted human life." The Court's verdict on this question is summed up in the following statement: "The unborn have never been recognized in the law as persons in the whole sense."

What the Court has tried to do has been to strike a fair balance between the State's two major interests in abortion—the duty to protect the woman's legal rights, which are limited and conditional, and the duty to protect the rights of the fetus, which are also limited and conditional. The rights of the woman become absolute only when her health is seriously at stake. The rights of the fetus become absolute only when it is viable; that is, when it has the capability of meaningful life outside the mother's womb.

On the basis of these principles, the Court has divided pregnancy into three stages. In the first three months, the woman has an unquestioned right to abortion if she can find a doctor who will perform the operation. After the third month, the State may regulate the right to abortion in accordance with medical estimates of the possible risks to the woman's health. However, in the third stage, when the unborn child becomes viable, and could live outside the womb, the State may deny the right of abortion entirely, unless medical judgment strongly advocates it.

Nobody doubted that this decisive legal judgment would increase the number of abortions in the United States. One estimate was that they would eventually climb to half the number of live births. In some other countries, the rates have actually gone far beyond that.

Three Major Implications

Let me now comment on three of the major implications of the Supreme Court verdict:

The verdict is not final. We must understand clearly that the subject is not closed to further discussion. Only a legal verdict has been passed. And the Court has been careful to point out that its verdict is based on what we like to call "the present state of our knowledge." The baffling question, "What is the value of unborn human life?" remains. And the search for an answer must go on, especially among the disciplines of medicine, philosophy, and theology which, as the Supreme Court reminds us, have so far failed to reach any consensus on the subject.

The Catholics, as you are aware, are campaigning vigorously to have the decision reversed. This will be very difficult to do legally; but they are very determined, and they are gaining some ground. As we have seen, the country was rushed into supporting abortion by a very vigorous propaganda campaign; and some thoughtful people are now beginning to have second thoughts.

Freedom of choice is the real issue. We must understand that our individual right to adopt whatever attitude we wish toward abortion has not been interfered with. If you believe that abortion is murder, you can go on holding that opinion; you can shout it from the housetops to everyone who will listen; you can join with like-minded people to propagate what you believe. What the new law does is not to take away your rights but to give to those who differ deeply from you the right not only to proclaim but also to practice what *they* believe. What this really signifies is the recognition that our society is not only democratic but also pluralistic, and we must be ready to put up with the inconveniences that this inevitably involves.

Of course it is very painful for people who think, as Catholics do, that abortion is murder, to see the law of this great country giving citizens the right of choice about committing the most serious of all crimes. But by no means do all Americans see the matter in this light. And in a democracy the law must represent the will of the people generally. If a decisive majority of Americans became convinced that the Catholics are right and were willing to stand up and be counted, there is no doubt whatever that the Supreme Court decision *could,* in time, be reversed.

Abortion counseling is an urgent need. The Supreme Court decision confronts us with the fact that the abortion decision, *Abortion: The Agonizing Decision* as I have called it in a book with that title, must increasingly be faced by large numbers of individual women. What the state is saying is: "Look, we are simply unable to settle these complicated ethical questions

for you. So you now have the freedom of choice. Henceforth
you may legally decide for yourself whether you want an abortion or whether you don't."

It was because I anticipated the Supreme Court decision that
I wrote my book on the subject. Amid all the raging controversy
about whether abortion is right or wrong, good or bad, no one
was giving much attention to the central figure in the drama—the
woman faced with the decision.

Only a few extremists can settle the question by saying that
abortion is always right or always wrong. What most of us
believe is that it is sometimes right and sometimes wrong,
depending on the circumstances. So, it usually comes down to
an individual decision. That is the woman's problem—to find
out what is the right decision for her personally. Some women
have no difficulty in making this decision. But for many others
it is so difficult that they can't do it without counseling help.

The campaigners for abortion insisted that the decision must
be arrived at between the woman and her doctor; and that
was the view the Supreme Court adopted. Unfortunately, this
overlooked the fact that the overwhelming majority of abortions
today are not sought on medical grounds at all, so that no
medical decision is involved. The role of the doctor is really
that of a technician. If the woman wants his help in reaching
an ethical decision, which normally requires hours of discussion,
the doctor can justifiably reply that he has neither the time
nor the training for such work.

My book was written because I saw it to be urgently necessary
that effective counseling services be provided for these women.
I am glad to report that great progress has now been made
in this direction, and such services have developed extensively
across the country.

Christians Confronting the Issues

Everyone who begins to study the abortion question soon
realizes how maddeningly complex it all is. I would be prepared
to say that this is the toughest ethical question the Christian

church has ever had to face or ever will have to face. I confess that one reason I wrote a book on the subject was that I wanted to think it through for myself and get clear in my own mind about where I personally stand.

Let me try to pinpoint the main issues with which we, as Christians, have to grapple. I won't try to give final answers, but will content myself with framing as clearly as I can the questions we have to be asking. There are three of them—the value of unborn life, the challenge of population control, and our changing sex morality.

As we struggle to deal with these issues, we are unfortunately offered very little direct help from the Bible. The people who lived in those far-off days simply didn't have to grapple with the problems we confront today. They neatly avoided most of our sexual problems by arranging for their boys and girls to be married soon after puberty. They had no hang-ups about sex itself—they thought it was good and necessary for all married men and women, which meant virtually *all* men and women, because everybody was expected to marry. They encouraged all married couples to have as many children as possible, because they had no population problems whatever. To the Hebrews, a woman who wanted an abortion would have been considered to be completely out of her mind. Motherhood was a woman's crowning glory, and the state of pregnancy was the greatest blessing that she could ever enjoy.

So Christians have to do some hard thinking to come up with convincing answers. Let us now examine the issues and see for ourselves how difficult it all is.

The value of unborn life. The ancient Hebrews believed that conception was the result of direct intervention, in which God showed his favor to the woman by opening her womb. This would suggest that they considered unborn life to be very precious—and they did. However, the Jewish rabbis believed that the fetus was not yet human life, but only *the promise of human life.* Their view was based on the statement in Genesis 2:7, which reads: "And the Lord God formed man of the dust of the ground, and breathed into his nostrils the breath of life; and man became a living soul." They took this to mean that the infallible sign of life was breathing. They knew, of course, that when a man dies, he ceases to breathe. So they concluded that when a child takes his first breath, he begins his life as a human being. If there *is* a biblical view on this matter, presumably that is it.

Throughout the history of the church, a tremendous controversy raged around the time when the soul was implanted in the body of the developing child. Some said that this happened at conception; some said it happened at the time of quickening, when the mother first felt her child move within her; some said it happened at birth. For the Catholic Church, the matter was not finally settled till December, 1965, at the Second Vatican Council, when Pope Paul officially declared that human life begins at the moment of conception.

The Catholic view is certainly logical, and in keeping with our new knowledge of human reproduction. Once the sperm and the ovum have fused together, a new, unique life begins; and every event that follows is no more than the progressive development of what came into existence at the moment of conception.

However, a great deal of development has to take place from this rudimentary beginning until the point at which the new life can survive independently; so it could be argued that this was not a complete, self-contained individual until it developed the capacity to exist by itself outside the womb. As we have seen, the Supreme Court decided, for the time being, that this would be considered as the point at which the fetus achieved the right to legal protection.

But of course the controversy will go on, *must* go on. We simply don't know the answers yet.

The challenge of population control. A few months ago, I spent a morning looking through a pile of journals that had accumulated. In one I found an article by a Catholic bishop about the shame and tragedy of all these abortions being done by doctors with the full approval of the state. He did not hesitate to denounce the whole business as savage brutality quite unworthy of a civilized Christian country. Immediately upon laying this down, I picked up a very authoritative article by a distinguished expert on world population and food supply. In the article he explained, with thorough documentation, how the earth's resources for producing food were now nearing their utmost limits; and the author did not hesitate to declare that unless we could cut back the human population, large numbers of people in the coming decades would be doomed to die miserably of starvation.

Here were two critical ethical issues in open confrontation with each other. Is it better, is it more Christian, to end human lives in the very early stages, swiftly and almost painlessly? Or to let them be born, only to die at some later time of starvation? It is a plain fact that attempts to control population throughout the world by persuading people to use contraceptives have been a dismal failure, and in country after country abortion has had to be introduced, either as an alternative to birth control, or as a back-up system when contraception fails.

The Catholics argue that we could produce more food if only we planned our resources better. No doubt that is true; but all it would do would be to postpone the inevitable crisis for a few more years. As it is, abortion doesn't fully solve the problem. But in countries like Japan, populations would already be out of control if national programs for legal abortion had not been introduced.

For the Catholics, of course, the problem is complicated further still because they not only condemn abortion, they condemn contraceptives too. One can only shudder in contemplating what the problem of world population might be like today if the Catholics had been able to persuade us all to give up the use of contraceptives. We can admire our Catholic friends for their strong convictions and for their single-minded devotion to what they believe. But as responsible members of the world community, at a time when further population increase appears to threaten us with stark disaster, can we in good conscience share their stand on this issue?

Our changing sex morality. Although abortions are often sought by married women who already have children and don't feel able to accept further pregnancies, we know also that many others represent sexual intercourse outside marriage, which is in violation of our traditional Christian code. So Christians could argue that if everyone behaved as he ought to behave, the need for abortion would be very much reduced.

It is easy enough to say this. But anyone who really knows what is going on among young people today is well aware that the chances of implementing this at the present time are very poor indeed. The trend for many years has been steadily in the opposite direction, and public opinion polls continue to show that more and more people in the United States are coming to regard sex outside marriage as inevitable, if not acceptable. For the foreseeable future, it would be totally unrealistic to predict any reversal of the present trend.

This puts many Christians, especially Christian parents, in a very difficult position. Are we to block measures to give contraceptives to unmarried girls, and thus increase the number of abortions? Or should we say, "We'd rather you didn't do this; but if you must, be responsible about it and take precautions"?

In my experience, the main reason why Christian girls seek abortions is out of fear of the religious wrath of their parents because they have become pregnant outside marriage. And the wrath of the parents is often caused by fear of the judgment of their fellow Christians. In all this I find little place for Christian compassion and little understanding of the complicated world in which young people are living today. In one case in which I was involved, the girl was deplorably ignorant about sex, and it turned out that her father had joined with others to close down a promising sex education program in the local high school.

Many a girl would gladly accept her pregnancy and give her child for adoption if her parents were not so afraid of public disgrace. Abortion has so depleted the adoption market today that there are thousands of loving homes. where babies that are being aborted would be welcome. Why should it be considered a disgrace for a married woman, who already has all the children she can raise and finds herself unexpectedly pregnant, to bear the child and give it for adoption? In China it has always been considered an act of generosity for a mother with children to give one of them to a woman who has none.

Another aspect of this perplexing ethical issue is that if abortion were not available, unmarried women might be less willing to run the risk of getting pregnant, and this would give some support to our traditional sex morality. However, I am afraid we can't assume that if the Supreme Court reversed itself and abortion were again declared illegal, it would cease to be available. No country has ever been able to prevent abortion by passing laws. Always the laws have been circumvented by illegal practitioners. And it would be much more difficult to prevent this now, after our experience of available abortion facilities, than it was before.

Conclusion

Let me try to sum up. The right of legal abortion has become a part of the American way of life. We may not like this, but it has happened, and we must come to terms with it.

We may have to tolerate abortion for a time, as a regrettable necessity. But surely we can and must find a better way. Surely our technology, which can split the atom and put men on the moon, will soon come up with an answer.

So we must, as Christians, confronting this serious and baffling problem, affirm that this is not the way we want to live, and it is not the way we want our friends and neighbors to live, nor the way we want Americans, or any other people, to live. We, therefore, declare our faith and our hope that a day will come (and may it come soon!) when men and women will be able to express and enjoy their sexuality without demeaning themselves or exploiting others; and when there will be no more problem pregnancies, no more avoidable abortions, and no more unwanted children.

13
Christianity and Women in the Future

Harry N. Hollis, Jr.

HELMER: Before all else you are a wife and mother.

NORA: That I no longer believe. I believe that before all else I am a human being, just as much as you are—or at least that I should try to become one.—Henrik Ibsen, *A Doll's House*, 1879

Just when men and women have the opportunity to mean more to each other than ever before, and when the world, the society, and that entity known as the family need them together, they are exploding apart.—Mary Calderone

The future will see women and men in the process of becoming the human beings God intends us to be. Thinking about the future is more than a parlor game. It is essential if we want to understand what may happen and how we can shape the forces that are at work in our culture.

The focus in this section will be on women specifically, but the impact of these trends on men and children will be considered also. Much attention will be given to sexual behavior in the future and it should be understood that "sex" is used in this chapter to refer to everything about a person that has to do with being a male or a female. Here are several trends which have already begun and will almost certainly continue in the future.

Scientific Developments

Scientific discoveries and technological developments will have a powerful impact and influence on the behavior of women and men.

Scientific technology has already had a strong impact on

behavior, and this trend will continue in the future. While some revolutions have moved slowly with less wide-ranging impact, the scientific-sexual revolution is moving rapidly. It affects not the periphery of life but the very nature of what it means to be human. It affects men and women. Here are some of the technological developments which scientists predict will take place in the near future. After these developments have been described, there will be a section to criticize those which are contrary to the Christian ideal for moral behavior.

Contraceptives. Additional refining of contraceptives in the future will assure nearly 100 percent effectiveness. Pregnancy will be strictly a matter of planning as the following developments take place: morning-after birth control pills; once-a-month pills; pills to make males infertile; shots to prevent pregnancy indefinitely; birth control implants under a woman's skin. Removing the risk of pregnancy will liberate many people for greater promiscuity. It will also give married couples freedom to enjoy intercourse by eliminating worry about having an unplanned pregnancy.

Test-tube fertilization. For some time artificial insemination has been practiced.[1] In the future, however, it will probably be a routine matter to take an egg from the female and fertilize it in a test tube. Then the fertilized egg can be placed in the womb. This means that a woman who could not conceive, due perhaps to blocked fallopian tubes, will become pregnant. A fertilized egg can be implanted in another woman's womb.

Embryo transplants. Suppose a woman gets pregnant but decides she does not want to carry the child. In the future, she may have the embryo transferred from her body to another woman who will carry and deliver the child for her. Women will be paid to provide this service. This practice will also mean that a woman unable to conceive can have an embryo transplanted from another woman's body to her own.

Ovary transplants. The future will also see the regular practice of transplanting ovaries in one woman from another, thus giving a woman who had been unable to get pregnant the chance to become instantly fertile.

Artificial wombs. In several parts of the world, scientists are working to perfect an artificial womb. Perhaps such a device will be completed for human fetuses. Although the artificial womb may have real value for premature babies, there are significant dangers in its use for the full nine months' development. Too little is known about proteins, hormones, and enzymes in natural pregnancy to prevent the accidental creation of psychological and biological monsters in these artificial devices.[2]

Should artificial wombs be perfected, however, there will be an almost total separation of sex and reproduction—even for parents! The ethical issues in the development of an artificial womb are frankly overwhelming. It would be possible for a woman to have a baby each month throughout her childbearing years! Minority groups could change their status into a majority one by arranging for their women to have four hundred babies apiece.

Frozen sperm banks. The technology is already available for storing sperm indefinitely through the process of freezing. It is likely that some famous and gifted people will be persuaded to contribute sperm to such banks for use through artificial insemination by those women who are willing to pay the fee to have a child by these outstanding individuals. A brilliant scientist, a successful athlete, or a movie hero may father thousands of children.

Asexual reproduction. As far-fetched as it now seems, the process of cloning may someday be a possibility. This is the technique by which a group of organisms is produced from a single common ancestor. For example, a cell taken from your body could be used to produce a number of bodies just like you (at least physically)! Should this method be perfected for humans someday, which I believe is extremely doubtful, sexual reproduction would be unnecessary. Needless to say, if cloning in humans becomes a reality, James Thurber's humorous question "Is sex necessary?" could be answered: "No, reproductive sex is no longer necessary!'"

Gender determination. Some scientists say that it will be possible to decide gender of offspring by taking a pill—pink for girl, blue for boy! (The ingredients, not the colors, are important!) "It's a girl!" can be announced before the child is conceived. This will have a far-reaching impact on our society. It could mean that the imbalance between the number of men and women will be corrected, thus reducing the number of women who have to live out later years without the companionship of men. Whether society will correct this imbalance remains to be seen.

The selection of gender can also have profound social, moral, and political effects, as sociologist Amitai Etzioni of Columbia University has pointed out.[3] Men vote Democratic more than women; so, a Democratic administration might propagandize people to have males! Women are more regular in church attendance; so, preachers might sermonize on the values of having female children. A male surplus without the influence of women might lead to a society with the rougher features of a frontier town and an increase in violence. Being male-oriented, lower economic class people might want more male children who in turn might seek to mate across class lines with females of a higher status group. It is also probable that a surplus of males would lead to increased homosexuality.

Responding to Scientific Developments

If only half of these scientific developments take place, the impact on behavior will be profound. How should we respond? Earlier we discussed a theology of human liberation which can guide us. What is required is to seek to determine how God is acting in these events and how we are called to respond.

God's creative activity continues. The creation is not yet complete. We can respond affirmatively to those scientific innovations in which we discern that God is working to improve the quality of human life. We can celebrate those developments which make it possible for infertile women to have children—

provided the dignity of procreation is protected. We can rejoice when a safe contraceptive allows a married couple to escape that fear of pregnancy which has blocked them from pleasure in intercourse.

At the same time, we can recognize that God also controls his creation and condemns the misuse of it. We are called to refrain from using scientific developments which are contrary to God's intentions. Everything that is scientifically possible is not morally permissible from a Christian point of view.

Exercising a spirit of humility, we are called to restrain scientific developments which contribute to the abuse of human life. Indiscriminate reproduction of human life in laboratories must be resisted. The frivolous use of the sperm of famous people to impregnate doting female admirers is really nothing more than artificial adultery. Also, males who take advantage of newly developed contraceptives to exploit a variety of sexual partners violate biblical teachings.

Acting as Redeemer, God is bringing his creation to completion. Scientific developments which reflect this movement toward wholeness in creation must be affirmed. If developments in the area of genetics enable us to eliminate birth defects or correct the imbalances between the number of males and females, we can respond with joy.

In redemption God gives us a model for the expression of love in all relationships. Scientific developments have virtually separated sex and reproduction. The fear of pregnancy has kept many married couples from enjoying the pleasure of intercourse which God intends. We can celebrate this enhancement of pleasure but not to the point where the important relation between sex and procreation is dismissed. Bearing a child is usually a fruit of love in marriage. To forget about the importance of reproduction in relation to sex is to miss something of the nature of sex. By understanding the community and fellowship which redemption makes possible, we can understand the nature of community between male and female and between parent and child.

Changing Family Patterns

Increasing participation in a wide variety of family patterns will affect men and women in society.

Today many people are experimenting with different family patterns. These experiments will increase in the near future. We will describe and then evaluate some of these patterns.

Unmarried patterns. A growing number of adults will decide not to marry. Being unmarried will be much more socially acceptable. The unmarried set will include:

The single celibate. For a variety of reasons some will not marry and will not have intercourse. Some single celibates may choose this state for *vocational* reasons, as Jesus did. Others will not marry because the opportunity will not present itself. In any case, these people can serve as a valuable corrective to our society's equation of salvation with sexual intercourse.

The single noncelibate. Many in the future will probably choose to stay single and have sexual intercourse with from one to many partners. This group will range from the playboy or playgirl to the men and women who choose not to marry but to have sexual intercourse with only one person.

Unmarried cohabitation. An increasing number of couples are living together without a marriage license. This practice seems to be gaining acceptance among college students and other young adults in our society.

By living together some couples seek to rebel against the traditional understanding of marriage and marital roles. A woman graduate student said: "I just can't imagine myself in the role of wife, and that is one reason I am much happier just living with Al without any thought of getting married." [4] In the light of such attitudes, it is probable that unmarried cohabitation is a pattern that will continue in the future.

Monogamy. How widespread will monogamy be in the future? The answer is unclear. Such forces as mobility, sexual permissiveness, and boredom are battering the practice of monogamy. Hopefully, movements to enrich marriage will bring new vitality to this marital pattern.

Traditional monogamy. This pattern, as used here, refers to one man and one woman staying married to each other for life and having intercourse only with each other. No doubt this pattern is now a minority one in our society. Yet, at best, it reflects the ideal set forth in the New Testament. The practice of a contagious monogamy reflecting the celebration of loving fidelity can bring this pattern into more widespread acceptance.

Celibate marriage. Surely this is a minor pattern which would not be mentioned at all except for its novelty. It has appeared at times in history. In the fourth century, Jerome practiced this pattern with two spiritual wives. More recently, the Shakers in this country advocated celibate marriage. It is described by Robert and Mary Joyce in their book, *New Dynamics in Sexual Love.* They look forward to the "virginal universe" of the afterlife by practicing a marriage now with love but no sexual intercourse.[5] Although this may serve as a corrective to an orgasm-oriented culture, it is certainly neither scriptural nor realistic.

Departures from monogamy. Present departures from traditional monogamy are likely to increase in the future, influencing behavior on a very wide scale.

Monogamy without sexual fidelity. This pattern is being called everything from "flexible monogamy" (Robert Francoeur) to "structured adultery" (Robert Rimmer). The "open marriage" concept of Nena and George O'Neill fits here also. Francoeur says that couples may stay married to each other for life but move from time to time into "satellite relations," which are "the brief but deep penetration of a comet into the couple's orbit, or more lasting intimate relations orbiting the couple at various levels."[6]

Serial marriage. Many people already practice this marital pattern by which they marry, divorce, and remarry perhaps several times. This is really a modified form of polygamy. There is little reason to believe that this practice will decrease in the future.

Three-step marriage. This classification has many variations, but it has been popularized by Alvin Toffler in *Future Shock*. He says that we will refer in the future not to a person's marital status but to his or her marriage career. The first stage of the career is the trial marriage which will occur once or several times during one's youth. In this stage a couple will get to know each other without having children.

In the second stage of the marriage career, the trial relationship will either be formalized or the couple will seek other mates. This second stage is when most couples will choose to have or adopt children. It will last until the children leave home for college or work.

The end of parenthood will mark the transition to the third stage of the marriage career. This will be the longest stage of marriage for many, although even here there will be several additional marriages for some.[7]

Temporary marriages, such as the three-step marriage described above, may be a prominent part of the future in this country.

Contract marriage. The auto operator's license which we apply for has to be renewed every two years or so. In the future there may very well be marriage licenses with similar requirements. In a contract marriage a couple will be given a marriage license for a specific number of years, perhaps three, four, or five. At the end of this period, the couple must renew the marriage, or it will automatically be dissolved. Other aspects of the marriage such as custody of children and disposition of property will also be spelled out clearly in the contract. The contract marriage may be an option chosen by an increasing number in the future.

Homosexual marriage. Already homosexual unions are widely practiced in America and in the future they may be legalized. Troy Perry, the homosexual pastor of the Metropolitan Community Church of Los Angeles, has officiated at more than 250 such unions.[8] Given the problems and tensions which homosexuals face in our society, it is likely that they will turn to marriage in the hope of finding security.

Homosexual couples will try to adopt children in the future, and this will lead to heated debates. Whether legal or informal, homosexual families will be a minority pattern in the future marital scene.

Polygamy. Although polygamy has been practiced widely in the past, there is some evidence that it may make a comeback in the future. It will take several forms.

Triangle marriage. In this arrangement there are usually two women and one man, although occasionally the ratio is reversed. Informal triangle relationships are now practiced in our society and this pattern will continue in the future. The practice of triangle marriage will lead to legal dilemmas, social adjustments (and maladjustments) for children in these families, and moral problems for churches to unravel.

Group marriage. At present people are experimenting with group marriage all over this country. The future will see even more of this. In group marriage three or more people join together in one household for sharing in every area of life from insurance to intercourse. These marriages are sometimes practiced in communes, although not all communal groups advocate group marriage. Given the dissatisfaction with nuclear family isolation plus the desire for novelty, group marriage will be a significant minority practice in the future.

Golden years polygamy. In an attempt to deal with the over-supply of females among the aged members of society, some are proposing and a few are practicing golden years polygamy. (Technically, this is polygyny, one man and several wives.) As the elderly increase in number and as they exercise "geritol power" to achieve their goals, it is conceivable that this marriage pattern may increase.

Responding to Changing Family Patterns

The variety of present and future marriage patterns calls for the most careful Christian response. Marriage is a part of God's intention for creation. The New Testament ideal for marriage is monogamy—one man and one woman in a covenant of fidelity and love for life. We are called to respond to the Creator by seeking to practice this ideal.

The best affirmation of monogamy will come in the way that we live. *Enriched marriages are evangelistic.* They do more for the cause of New Testament monogamy than words of admonition can ever do by themselves.

God is also acting as Judge to condemn the abuse of marriage. Built into the very nature of things is his control. When we practice patterns contrary to his will, we suffer the anxiety that comes with lack of genuine fulfillment. Adultery will be judged by God whether it be called "structural adultery" or "satellite relations" or "open marriage outside companionships." We can respond to God's activity as Judge by accepting his condemnation of the abuse of marriage relationships.

How shall we respond to homosexual marriages? Clearly such unions must be rejected as contrary to God's intention for the structuring of society. This does not mean that we should be arrogant or act in a holier-than-thou manner toward homosexuals. Instead, we can be both firm and compassionate in teaching that homosexuality misses God's intention for sexual behavior. And, in a spirit of humility, we can help homosexuals get professional therapy. We can also work to change those family and social pressures which so often contribute to a homosexual life-style.

What about singles? God calls some for marriage and some for celibacy. Others find themselves without a mate due to death or divorce. The important fact for all of us, in whatever marital status, is that we pattern our relations to others after the nonexploitative, self-giving love of Christ. Salvation is not based on being married or unmarried; it is based on our relation to God in Jesus Christ.

Clearly God's redemptive activity teaches us how to respond to changing marriage patterns. In the relation of Christ and his church we have a pattern of love and fidelity for our own marriage relationship. The truth is that the practice of a loveless monogamy has led many to look for alternate patterns. Children of such unhappy marriages are now looking for a better way.

That better way can be found if Christians will respond to the Redeemer by practicing a contagious monogamy full of joy, fidelity, and love. This is the best hope to call people back from sub-Christian alternatives.

Sexual Pluralism

In the future sexual pluralism will characterize the American culture.

A variety of sexual life-styles will be found in America in the future. Government will take less interest in the private sexual practices of individuals. Anonymity and mobility will enable people to leave their immediate community and do just about what they want to away from the eyes of anyone who knows them. Increasingly, sexual behavior will not be governed by laws and social pressure. If people behave, it will be because they want to. Society will be more tolerant of deviations from community norms.

The emancipated woman of the future "will lead the way to a more realistic understanding of the nature of sex," according to Duane Mehl.[9] She sees the advent of a new "romanticism which allows for both the potential good and evil of sexual expression." Also, a "new ethic will emerge, not from puritan codes nor religious systems once accepted by society, but from a mutual fear of and distaste for decadence; and, may I add, often from nervous exhaustion."[10]

Sociologist Ira Reiss has written that America is moving "toward a Scandinavian type of system of sex standards, with key emphasis on the association of sex and affection and the quality of interpersonal relationship."[11] Although the church has been strongly against premarital sexual permissiveness in the past, Reiss predicts that "the Protestant clergy especially in the wealthier denominations, will take rather liberal positions on sex and here too lead young people toward greater permissiveness rather than blocking that development."[12]

The frantic preoccupation with sex today reflects the immaturity of a culture with sexual hang-ups. As these hang-ups diminish, sex will assume its proper place in the behavior of most people. Sexual problems will never disappear. Some people will continue to express sex in unhealthy ways in the future. But the cultural preoccupation with sex will subside.

In the future, people may wonder why there has been so much fuss over sex. According to Marshall McLuhan and George Leonard: "Sex may well be regaining some of its traditional cool. It is still a three-letter word, in spite of the efforts of its four-letter relatives to 'hot it up.' This is not to say that the future will be sexless. Far from it, generations yet to come may very well find all of life far more erotic than now seems possible." [13]

This means that the contemporary obsession with pornography will probably diminish. There will always be too much pornography in society but the pornographers are running out of encores. The future will see a constant battle between the pornographers' approach to sex and a Christian approach. There may be cycles in the arts in the future that run from neo-puritanism to sexual libertinism, but hopefully a more healthy Christian approach to sex will prevail.

Responding to Sexual Pluralism

Sexual pluralism requires a continuing response from Christians who are concerned about the quality of life in society. The model of God's activity and human response instructs us in the kind of approach that can be made toward sexual pluralism.

God, acting as Creator, has made us sexual beings for the enrichment and fulfillment of our lives. Any actions which are in keeping with God's intention for sexual expression can be affirmed. Actions which demean sex and contribute to unhealthy expression are to be rejected.

In the midst of an explosion of knowledge about sex, we are called to protect the mystery of sex intended by the Creator.

We know more about the physiology, psychology, and sociology of sex than ever. But sex cannot be reduced to charts or statistics. The Creator has built mystery and wonder into sex. Wholesome modesty must be maintained, while suspicious prudery can be exposed as an anti-sexualism contrary to the will of the Creator.

God acts as Judge to make self-defeating those sexual styles which go against his intention for human behavior. The restrictions of the past have been replaced by new compulsions which keep people from being truly free in their sexual expressions.[14] A new "thou shalt" legalism to conform to permissiveness threatens the freedom of both male and female today. Remaining a virgin until marriage today often requires one to defend this choice against criticism and pressure of friends.[15] We are called to respond to these compulsions not with counter compulsions but by sharing the good news of genuine freedom in a life patterned after Jesus Christ.

Some use sex as a means by which to retreat permanently from the larger community. They are tempted, in light of the complex problems of life, to set up a private kingdom in which sex is elevated to the place of a god. As both work and politics continue to be dehumanized, there is an increasing temptation to depend on the privacy of life to compensate.[16] Sexual expression cannot stand the burden of divinity. It will break down under the load, bringing disaster to those who seek salvation through it. We are called to respond to God's judgment by condemning this misuse of sex.

Responding to God's activity as Redeemer means an affirmation of sexual expression which promotes love. By demonstrating in our lives the love revealed in Christ, we can offer an alternative to sexual practices which lead to anxiety and frustration. Redemption means hope. What many people need is the hope that we are moving toward a time when they will not be exploited sexually.

What is the role of the church as a community of hope in a culture with sexual pluralism? What part will it have in the future of sex? In spite of all dire predictions to the contrary,

of Jesus teaches us that love is not a petty guarding of our rights but a joyful giving of ourselves to others. It is not only justice that women's liberation movements must seek between the sexes, but also love. In the midst of a culture where many are seeking liberation, Christians have good news to share. Jesus Christ brings true freedom and fulfillment to all people. This is the refreshing word that is breaking in upon our world. We are called to share this good news that there is Christian freedom for women—and other human beings. In Christ we can all be free!

Notes

1. Artificial insemination is the introduction of semen into the genital tract of the female by artificial means.

2. Robert Francoeur, "Technology and the Future of Human Sexuality" in *To Create a Different Future,* edited by Kenneth Vaux (New York: Friendship Press, 1972), p. 91.

3. Helen Colton, *Sex After the Sexual Revolution* (New York: Association Press, 1972), p. 245.

4. Quoted by George Thorman, "Cohabitation," *The Futurist,* VII (December, 1973), p. 253.

5. Francoeur, *op. cit.,* p. 103.

6. *Ibid.,* p. 99.

7. Alvin Toffler, *Future Shock* (New York: Random House, 1970), pp. 224 ff.

8. Ronald M. Enroth and Gerald E. Jamison, *The Gay Church* (Grand Rapids: William B. Eerdmans Publishing Company, 1974), p. 85.

9. Duane Mehl, *Motive,* XXVII (October, 1966), p. 29.

10. *Ibid.*

11. Ira Reiss, "The Sexual Renaissance: A Summary and Analysis," *The Journal of Social Issues,* XXII (April, 1966), p. 123.

12. *Ibid.,* p. 133.

13. Marshall McLuhan and George B. Leonard, "The Future of Sex," *Look,* XXXI (July 25, 1967), p. 63.

14. Harvey Cox, "Sexuality and Responsibility," in *Sexual Ethics and Christian Responsibility,* John C. Wynn, ed. (New York: Association Press, 1970), pp. 30-31.

15. *Ibid.,* pp. 35-36.

16. *Ibid.,* p. 31.

17. Toffler, *op. cit.,* pp. 216-217.

18. Marshall McLuhan and George B. Leonard, *op. cit.,* p. 57.

19. *Ibid.*

20. *Ibid.,* p. 58.

21. Vance Packard, *The Sexual Wilderness* (New York: Van Rees Press, 1968), p. 119.

Questions for Further Study

Discussing the issues raised in this book can help raise consciousness about freedom for all human beings. A group of interested females and males might meet together weekly (or less often) and discuss one chapter at each meeting. The group can begin with the questions suggested here and then turn to those matters of special interest in each chapter.

CHAPTER 1: "Women and the Family in the Bible"
1. What can we learn from Jesus about the treatment of women? Why do the Maces begin the biblical section with a discussion of Jesus and women?
2. How were Hebrew wives generally treated in Old Testament times? Where Hebrew women considered subordinate to men? Why?
3. What do the Maces have to say about Paul's treatment of women?
4. Some do not think the Bible is relevant to the predicament of contemporary women. Do you agree? Why?

CHAPTER 2: "Changing Responsibilities of Women in the Church"
1. What part do *kinder* (children), *kleiden* (clothing), *kuche* (kitchen), and *kirche* (church) play in the life of modern women? Is this changing?
2. Why are there not more women in places of denominational leadership?
3. What arguments are used to support and to oppose the ordination of women as ministers? What is your position?
4. What does Dr. Anders mean by "spiritual feminism"? Will it change the churches?

CHAPTER 3: "A Theology for Human Liberation"
1. Is it valid to talk about a theology of women? Why or why not?
2. How can women celebrate their femaleness? How can men celebrate their maleness? How can both sexes celebrate their humanity?
3. Why is woman so often linked to the Fall?
4. Can Jesus liberate women? How?

CHAPTER 4: "Women and the Family in Christian History:
1. What were the major ideas about women in the period of the early church?
2. What part did eschatology (the doctrine of "last things") play in developing attitudes toward family life?

3. Discuss the Middle Ages' attitudes toward women.
4. Why did the Reformation not bring greater changes in the status of women?

CHAPTER 5: "A History of Women's Liberation Movements"
1. Why does Dr. Anders begin with early civilizations in her discussion of a history of women's liberation movements?
2. What gave rise to "the New Women's Movement"?
3. Discuss the points of consensus in the manifestos of women's movements.
4. What do you predict will happen to feminism in the church?

CHAPTER 6: "Myths About Men and Women"
1. Why are myths about males and females so persistent? How do these myths get started? How can they be exploded?
2. Evaluate the "sugar and spice" and the "puppy-dog tail" myths. What are the innate differences between males and females?
3. Discuss the matriarchy myth.
4. What additional myths about men and women have you encountered in our society?

CHAPTER 7: "A Christian Critique of Institutional Discriminations Against Women"
1. Why is discrimination against women so widespread in business? How soon will significant changes come?
2. Is there governmental discrimination against women in your community?
3. How are the many faces of the mass media bringing about changes for women?
4. What can be done about stereotypes in commercial advertising?

CHAPTER 8: "Women and the Family in Today's World"
1. The question is often asked: "What do women want?" How do the Maces answer? What is your answer?
2. Why have the rewards of homemaking diminished today?
3. Evaluate the statement of Margaret Mead that parents stand helpless and frustrated while the mass media raise their children.
4. Respond to Dr. Jessie Bernard's research findings that seem to indicate that marriage today is much better and healthier for men than for women.

CHAPTER 9: "Women, Men, and Marriage"
1. How can a companionship family be developed? Can a couple be trained to be true companions?
2. How can a couple shift from fixed roles to shared roles?
3. Discuss ways that a couple can practice equity in planning their work responsibilities.
4. Will women's liberation help or harm marriages? Explain.

CHAPTER 10: "Women and the Sexual Revolution"
   1. Is a sexual revolution taking place in America? What evidence can you cite to support your answer?
   2. What can be done about pornography?
   3. Have scientific developments improved the quality of sexual expression?
   4. Do you agree that "voluntarily having no children is usually unwise"?

CHAPTER 11: "A Christian Approach to Women and Health"
   1. Are American women healthier than men?
   2. What can the church do about addiction to alcohol and other drugs among women?
   3. What problems do women face because the medical field is male-dominated?
   4. How can Christian activism help women secure better health?

CHAPTER 12: "A Christian Understanding of Abortion"
   1. What factors led to greater acceptance of abortion in America?
   2. Why does Dr. Mace suggest that the Supreme Court verdict about abortion is not final?
   3. Should abortion be used to help check the population explosion?
   4. What can be done to diminish the number of abortions in America?

CHAPTER 13: "Christianity and Women in the Future"
   1. Discuss ethical issues related to: test-tube fertilization, artificial wombs, and embryo transplants.
   2. What kind of future do you see for marriage in America? How can enriched marriages be evangelistic?
   3. What can the church do about sexual permissiveness?
   4. What are your predictions about the future for women and men?

'°TE DUE

Christian freedom for women and other human beings / Harry N. Hollis, Jr. ... [et al.]. — Nashville : Broadman Press, [1975]

192 p. ; 21 cm.

ISBN 0-8054-5552-3

1. Women in Christianity—Addresses, essays, lectures. 2. Women—Addresses, essays, lectures. I. Hollis, Harry.

BV639.W7C45   261.8'34'12   74-21566
                                                               MARC

Library of Congress   75